MORAG – MYSELF OR MOTHER-HEN?

DAVENPORT

Sers **IN SEARCH OF A THERAPIST**

Series Editors: Michael Jacobs and Moira Walker

T **MORAG – MYSELF OR MOTHER-HEN?**

A *Edited by Moira Walker*

P OPEN UNIVERSITY PRESS
Buckingham • Philadelphia

Open University Press
Celtic Court
22 Ballmoor
Buckingham
MK18 1XW

and 1900 Frost Road, Suite 101
Bristol, PA 19007, USA

First published 1995

A catalogue record of this book is available from the British Library

ISBN 0–335–19224–6 (pbk)

Library of Congress Cataloging-in-Publication Data

Morag, myself or mother hen? / edited by Moira Walker.
     p.   cm. — (In search of a therapist)
    Includes bibliographical references and index.
    ISBN 0–335–19224–6 (pbk.)
    1. Psychotherapy—Case studies.   I. Walker, Moira, 1948– .
II. Series.
    RC465.M67   1995
    616.89'14 —dc20
                               95–9568
                                 CIP

Typeset by Graphicraft Typesetters Limited, Hong Kong
Printed in Great Britain by St Edmundsbury Press,
Bury St Edmunds, Suffolk

CONTENTS

THE EDITOR AND CONTRIBUTORS

Roxane Agnew is a clinical psychologist working in a community mental health team serving adult mental health in Leicester. She specializes in focused expressive psychotherapy for clients with over-controlled emotions and has a research interest in therapeutic relationships.

Windy Dryden is Professor of Counselling at Goldsmiths College, University of London. He has authored or edited over 85 books, including *Rational-Emotive Counselling in Action* (New York: Sage Publications, 1990). His major interests are in rational-emotive behaviour therapy, eclecticism and integration in therapeutic practice, and increasingly in writing short, accessible self-help books for the general public, such as his latest, *Ten Steps to Positive Living* (London: Sheldon, 1994).

Paul Holmes is a consultant child and adolescent psychiatrist in the National Health Service, and a psychodramatist and trainer in private practice. He is co-editor with Marcia Karp of *Psychodrama: Inspiration and Technique* and with Marcia Karp and Michael Watson of the book *Psychodrama Since Moreno: Innovations in Theory and Practice* (London: Tavistock/Routledge, 1994). His book *The Inner World Outside: Object Relations Theory and Psychodrama* (London: Tavistock/Routledge, 1992) reflects his interest in the integration of the theories of psychodrama, psychoanalysis and family therapy.

Arthur Jonathan is a UKCP-registered existential psychotherapist in private practice. Originally a senior lecturer in education at Goldsmiths College, he subsequently completed an MA in psychotherapy and counselling and the advanced diploma in existential psychotherapy at the School of Psychotherapy and Counselling, Regent's College, where he is now a senior lecturer and director of the certificate programme. He is a founding member of the Society for Existential Analysis. He is currently Chair of the Humanistic and Integrative Psychotherapy Section of UKCP.

Anthea Millar is an Adlerian counsellor, trainer and supervisor. She has set up an Adlerian counselling course in Cambridge, on which she tutors. She is author of *Introduction to Counselling Skills* (Cambridge: Daniels, 1991) and *Counselling and Cooperation in the Classroom* (Cambridge: Daniels, 1991), and co-author with Angela Cameron of *Active Listening: A Counselling Skills Approach* (Cambridge: Daniels, 1994).

Peter Savage was educated, as a mature student, at the Universities of Oxford and Manchester. He is a professional lecturer, and trained with the National College of Hypnosis and Psychotherapy, of which he became principal in 1987. He is an external tutor in hypnotherapy to the Institute of Advanced Nursing Education at the Royal College of Nursing, a member of the National Register of Hypnotherapists and Psychotherapists, and on the UK Council for Psychotherapy's National Register of Psychotherapists.

Moira Walker is head of the counselling service at the University of Leicester. She is a UKCP-registered psychotherapist, and a writer with a special interest in working with women and with abuse survivors. She also supervises and trains counsellors and psychotherapists.

And Morag, whose contribution forms the core of this book, has for obvious reasons to remain anonymous, although much of her life story is told in full in these pages.

MICHAEL JACOBS AND MOIRA WALKER

SERIES EDITORS' PREFACE

Take five clients, and for each client take five or six therapists. How will the therapists, or in one case the supervisors as well, understand and work with the following situations?

Charlie is a 40-year-old secretary to a Trade Union official, married with three children:

I think of myself as someone who lacks self-confidence and feels she always has to apologize for herself, and I'm very insecure. The mildest row with my husband and I think he's going to leave me, and he finds that very irritating, I think. Understandably. I would. Having thought about it, I blame my mother for that. I use the word 'blame' quite consciously, because all the while I very much got the impression when I was young that she didn't love me and doesn't love me. I think of myself as unlovable.

Jitendra is a male Indian psychiatrist, separated from his Irish wife:

One thing that . . . interests me and sometimes worries me is my early years, my childhood years. I have very few memories of anything before the age of six or five, but I am sure that they have left some legacy behind, a significant legacy, and sometimes I have deep feelings of sadness or complexity or ambivalence which are not immediately ascribable to events happening around me. And I wonder what these . . . what this augurs? I think a therapist might . . . help me in this area. The other area that I am wanting to understand is the dynamics of a large extended family . . . I would like to understand a little bit more about what affects a person's growing up in that context.

Morag is an accountant, the director of a catering business, a mother, stepmother and partner:

> I feel that James wants me to be in the house, to be there because his children are there, and the family's there. He's quite happy to go off and play rugby on Sunday but he likes me being there, being the mother-hen . . . I get quite cross, that he keeps trying to push me into the traditional role. I don't feel I've got on as far as I could have done had I been a man, because I had to work twice as hard as everybody else to get where I got, . . . I feel OK always wanting to do something, but it does seem to cause quite a lot of conflict in my life. I feel, 'Is it right that I should always be wanting something new to go at, some new challenge? Should I just be accepting the way I am?'

Peta is an unemployed art teacher living in London:

> I've got a problem with men. At least that's the way that I conceptualize it for the moment. I don't know whether it's a problem with other things as well, but over the last few weeks, particularly – which is a different thing from deep background, I suppose you'd say – some issues seem to have come into my mind that are to do with the fact that I am a woman and they men . . . It's rather difficult to know where to start, except that I feel very self-conscious and rather uncomfortable about the fact that I must also tell you that I'm a feminist. And also that my father was emotionally very distant.

Ruth was abused as a young girl. She wants to hold her male therapist. What can he say when she says to him:

> Your reaction was – or I perceived it as being – a stand-off, and be cold to it, and not let anything happen, which obviously I understand; but I think it just highlighted that my desire . . . is not going to be matched by anyone else's. How can I communicate where I'm at, and help somebody else to understand that, and not necessarily to capitulate to me but just to be understanding?

This unique series of books takes a client's story, his or her presenting difficulties, the current situation, and some of the history from an initial session, recorded verbatim and printed in full for the reader to use. The session has in each case been presented to five or six different therapists. They address their questions to the client, and explain in each book how they understand the client, how they want to work with the client, what further information they requested,

and in the light of what they know, how they forecast the course
of therapy. The reader is presented with five or six possible interpretations and working methods to compare and contrast, with a final
telling response from the client and the editor on each of the
therapists.

This series takes a further step forward from the comparative approaches of Rogers and others on film, or the shorter case vignettes
in the *British Journal of Psychotherapy*, which have both been deserv-
edly so popular with students and practitioners alike. All the therapists start with precisely the same information, which comes from
a largely non-directed initial hour with four real clients. The reader
can see in detail how each therapist takes it from there. How they
share similar and contrasting insights and interpretations of the
same person proves a remarkable and fascinating study of how different therapists work.

The final volume in the series goes a step further and submits one
session of the editor's work with a long-term client to five different
supervisors. How do they interpret the verbatim material? What
questions do they want to ask the therapist? How do they advise the
therapist how to proceed? In this detailed insight into the work of
a therapist and supervisors from different orientations, the reader
gets an in-depth view of the value of supervision.

The five volumes in the series are entitled *Charlie – An Unwanted
Child?*, *Peta – A Feminist's Problems with Men*, *Morag – Myself or Mother-
hen?*, *Jitendra – Lost Connections* and, finally, *In Search of Supervision*.

1 THE EDITORS

IN SEARCH OF THE CLIENT

Just how different is the approach used by a therapist from one particular training society from that of a therapist from another orientation? In recent years, there has been much more interest in comparing approaches than in competing approaches. It is sometimes suggested that different methods may suit different clients, or even that therapists tend to select out the clients they can best work with.

There have been other attempts to demonstrate the way in which therapists from different schools might work with the same client. For many years, the two series of short films *Three Approaches to Psychotherapy*, the first made with Rogers, Perls and Ellis and the client 'Gloria', and the second with Rogers, Shostrom and Lazarus and the client 'Kathy', were well used in counselling training. Raymond Corsini tried a similar comparison in print, in the book *Five Therapists and a Client* (Itasca, Illinois: F.E. Peacock Publishing, 1991), although in our opinion his book is marred by several weaknesses. In the first place, the client is a fictional case, and the first session therefore written entirely from Corsini's imagination – drawing presumably on clients he has known. Second, there are inconsistencies even within the first session, making the case less plausible. Third, each of the responding therapists is asked to imagine how the therapy would go, similarly writing their own dialogue. This gives them *carte blanche* to develop the case along the lines they want their therapy to pursue, which demonstrates the validity of their approach, and in each case ends up with success for their method with the client.

We wanted to approach the question of how different therapists might work with the same client from yet another angle. We wanted a real client, not a fictional situation as in Corsini's work, but more perhaps as Gloria and Kathy were in the sessions recorded with Rogers and other therapists. In this series, we wanted to preserve the anonymity of the client, which a video or film cannot do. We also wanted to avoid what we believe inevitably happened in *Three Approaches to Psychotherapy*. The client is seen by three therapists in turn, but may be influenced in her responses to the second and third by what has happened in previous interview(s). We wanted all the therapists to start with precisely the same information, and to see how they might take it from there. In this introduction, we explain how we went about that and subsequent parts of the task.

Finding the clients

We used various contacts throughout the country to identify potential participants in the project, providing an outline of the method to be used. We invited applications from people who had never been in therapy before, since we wanted to avoid the contamination of their material by what might otherwise have been influenced from a previous therapist's interpretations. As it turned out, we learned rather late in the day that one of the clients had had a very short period of counselling with a person-centred counsellor, but over a rather different presenting issue to the one she brought to her first session with us.

After meeting those who were interested, and explaining to them the method and the safety features which we describe in more detail below, we invited them to return a consent form if they wished to continue. Their consent did not bind them to final agreement to take part, until the point at which they agreed to release the material from the first session. They could withdraw at any moment up to that point at which the therapists would receive their material, and were therefore committed to work on it. We for our part promised absolute confidentiality and anonymity (not even the publishers would know their names and addresses), and control by the client over any material which could lead to identification. We also asked the client to accept that we could not take them on for therapy, and that we could not be held responsible for their therapy, although we would endeavour to find them the most appropriate therapy if, during the course of our contact with them throughout the project, they so desired it. We also made it clear that we might not use their material, since we would be seeing more people than the series could use.

Several dropped out at this stage. Seven people responded that they wished to take part, and between us the two editors arranged to meet those who agreed to take part for an initial interview. We arranged to meet for up to an hour, recording the interviews. We told them as we started that we would say very little, except to prompt them to say a little more where we felt they might value such a response. Some were more fluent than others, but we hope that we did not over-influence the course of the interviews. It was to be the client's agenda which each presented to us, and through us, to their six therapists. Our own interventions are recorded word for word in the record of the first session.

Of the seven interviews, three proved unsuitable for use in the project. All three were as interesting as those we finally chose, but two of them proved too similar as presenting issues to another which we already hoped to be able to use. The third interview concerned us both because of the age of the client, and also because our understanding of the material concerned us. We felt it wiser to leave the client with natural defences. We had to be as sure as we could be from one non-directed interview that our client would survive any of the stresses that might arise in the course of such a project.

We finished with four tapes from which to work, and we checked with the four clients that they still wanted to proceed before we transcribed the tapes. The second chapter of each volume in the series is a word-for-word transcript of the first interview. The only changes that have been made are to certain possible identifying features. These have been altered with the agreement and with the assistance of the client. The alterations made were internally consistent with the client's presenting story.

Once the transcript was prepared, it was sent to the client to be checked, particularly with regard to any further alterations necessary to disguise actual identity. We did not allow the client to change his or her mind about what had been said, unless to facilitate a disguise of identity, or where there was a clear typing error. Once more we made it clear that the client could withdraw from the project if he or she wished to. Only if the client was completely satisfied with the account which was to be sent to the therapists, and which would form the key chapter of the book, was the client then asked to assign the copyright of the material to the editors.

Finding therapists

Simultaneously, we started to look for therapists who could represent, at least in their theoretical position, the different approaches we wished to include in each volume. We wanted to find distinct methods or schools for each client, and where possible to have three

male and three female therapists. Taking the four initial books in
the series together, we hoped to represent every major school of
therapy. Suggestions were gathered from our own contacts, and
therapists who were unable to accept an invitation were asked to
suggest a colleague who might. In some cases we asked a professional society to nominate one of its members.

For the most part our task went smoothly enough, and the response we had was encouraging. Many of those who accepted our
invitation quite rightly had one major reservation, that their work
with clients depended partly (or in some cases largely) upon the face-
to-face relationship, and working with its nuances. They accepted
that in this case it was impossible to have that particularly subjective experience informing their work, although some more directly
than others asked for our own observations, feelings and intuition
in some of the questions they asked of us. This concern – a lack of
direct contact with the client – was also given as the reason why
some of those we approached to represent psychoanalytic psychotherapy turned down our invitation. This was the most difficult
space to fill, although other reasons were also given, each one genu-
ine in its own way. We began to wonder whether there was some
resistance from therapists in this orientation to 'going public'. But
perhaps it was pure coincidence that we had no such problems with
any of the other therapies, including other psychodynamic approaches. We occasionally had a refusal, but nearly always with the
suggestion of someone else we might ask, who then accepted.

The work on this volume was particularly marked by the death of
Michael Watson, who was taking part in Morag's therapy as the
psychodrama therapist. He was enthusiastic about the project, keen
to take part, and supplied the editors with the detailed instructions
for taking Morag through the Social Atom Exercise. This was sent
back to him just a few days before he died, when the editors did not
know that he was ill. He was unable to take this work with Morag
any further. His friend and colleague in the British Psychodrama
Association, Paul Holmes, took over the work from the point which
he had reached, and his chapter is dedicated to Michael's memory.

Responding to the client

Our therapists were told, in the original invitation, that having read
the material they would have the opportunity to ask further questions of the client, through us the editors. We felt that it would be
disruptive for the client to meet each of the six therapists in turn,
and that it would make the chances of identification rather greater,

since it has remained the case that only the editors know who the clients really are. We were also concerned that we should continue to monitor what was happening for the client in the whole process. This is a person's life and story that we all have responsibility for, and while we wished the therapists to be totally honest, we also wished to ensure the clients survived, without unnecessary damage to them.

The therapists were therefore invited to ask for further information in order to address the headings we had suggested to them for their chapters to be consistent with one another. We all recognized, on both sides, that therapists would not bluntly ask questions of a client, but that some would take a life history early on, while others would expect such information to emerge during the course of therapy. We had to assume that there was certain information each therapist would hope to receive before the end of therapy. We were unprepared for just how much the therapists wanted to ask, and what we had thought would be a simple second interview proved to be more arduous and searching than either we or the clients could have imagined.

Most of the therapists sent long lists of areas they wished to explore further. Some sent questionnaires or psychometric tests. They asked in some cases for drawings, or for our own personal responses to the client. We were both involved in Michael Watson's request for us to conduct the Social Atom Exercise with Morag, Moira Walker as the director, Michael Jacobs as the recorder. We collated the sets of questions so that they could be asked in a more or less natural sequence, putting questions from different therapists about particular aspects of the client's life or history in the same section of the interview, or where they were nearly identical asking them together. Although each therapist only received back the information for which they had clearly asked, where questions were almost the same, they received the same material and a reprint of the other therapist's question. Similar areas were addressed, but very few questions were actually close enough to be asked together. In a few instances, where the client referred back to an answer already given to one therapist, we supplied that information as necessary to a second therapist whose question had evoked this reference.

The interviews with our clients at this stage took several hours – we met at least twice, in two cases three times, and once four times. We carefully monitored how much the client could take, and asked periodically how much more they wanted to answer at that session. The questions were often searching and they sometimes gave rise to painful feelings and uncomfortable memories, although our experience was that none of the clients found this anti-therapeutic. They and we were stretched more than we might have anticipated, and we valued the immense thoughtfulness which the therapists had put into their questions, and the clients put into their answers.

Inevitably, there was a long gap between the first interview and the subsequent series of separate interviews that took place much closer together. The original problems may have shifted a little, sometimes being slightly less troubling, sometimes slightly more so. The time lapse did not otherwise have much significance, except in the thought which each client had given to their own original material in the intervening period. Their own silent working on this material probably made their responses to the questions rather more full. Certainly many thousands of words were transcribed in each case, once again with the agreement of the client, before being sent off to the individual therapists. In all but one instance, the client was seen by the same person throughout. In Morag's case, her original interview was with Michael Jacobs. To share the task of editing the four client volumes, it was necessary for her to be allocated to Moira Walker for the second and subsequent interviews and collation of material, although, as already indicated, the second set of interviews were rounded off well, since both of us were involved in her Social Atom Exercise.

The therapists' task

The therapist's brief was to use the original material, and supplementary information which they received from their questions and other 'tests' or questionnaires, to write an assessment of the client along the following lines, which form the main headings of each chapter.

1 A brief description of their own training background, and their therapeutic approach. Even though they are known to represent a particular orientation (e.g. person-centred), we recognize that each therapist has particular ways of working, which might draw upon aspects of other approaches. What is important is to see how an actual therapist rather than a theoretical therapy works in practice.

2 The second section consists of the further questions which the therapist asked of the client through the editor therapist, and the responses they feel are relevant to their understanding of the client. Phrases such as 'When I met the client' refer to meeting the client via the editor. For reasons that have been explained already, none of the therapists made contact with or spoke directly to the clients.

3 The therapist's assessment of and reaction to the client – how he
   or she understands the client and the material the client has
   presented. This takes different forms, in line with the particular
   therapeutic approach, empathic identification with the client,
   counter-transference towards the client, etc. The therapists have
   been asked to provide indications or evidence of how they arrived
   at any formulation they might make, even if it is inevitably somewhat speculative.
4 The next section outlines therapeutic possibilities – indications
   and contraindications in the client and in the therapist/therapy,
   in that it may or may not be helpful for that particular client.
5 The fifth section hypothesizes the course of therapy – what form
   it might take, the methods, the contract, the theoretical approach
   in practice, and any shifts in approach that might be necessary to
   accommodate the particular client.
6 Next, the therapist suggests possible problem areas and how they
   might be resolved. We have asked that potential difficulties are
   faced and not given a favourable gloss if it seems the client might
   not prove amenable to some aspects of a particular approach.
7 The therapist is asked to explain his or her criteria for success in
   this case and to try to predict how far these may be met. Aware
   of the positive outcome in all Corsini's therapists' accounts, we
   asked the therapists not to predict a totally positive outcome if
   they had any doubts about it.
8 Each therapist concludes with a short summary and a short reading list for those interested in pursuing his or her approach.

The final stage

As the therapists returned their assessments of the client, and their
account of how they would work with him or her, the material was
passed over to the client to read. When all six assessments had been
received, we met with the client for a penultimate session, to discuss
the content of the final chapter together, before the editor wrote it.
While it had been generally obvious throughout just how much the
clients had gained from the process, their own final assessment both
of the therapists and of the process is therefore available at the end
of each book. We intend to meet with them one more time, when
the book is published, to complete our part in their own search for
change and understanding.

To them and to the therapists who took part we owe a great debt.
They have each in their own way demonstrated a deep commitment to each other, and have furnished the reader with a unique

opportunity of comparing not only their own approaches, but also the reader's response to the client with their own. (Following the client's original story in Chapter 2, the reader will find space in Chapter 3 to record ideas, questions and feelings, with suggested questions that are similar to those we first addressed to the therapists.) The therapists have also shown a willingness to work cooperatively in a project which will do much to advance the comparative study of the many different approaches and nuances which the psychotherapy and counselling world embraces. This series shows how little need there is for competition, and how the different therapies can complement one another in the service of those who seek their help.

2 MORAG

MYSELF OR MOTHER-HEN?

Morag is tall, slim, casually dressed and much of the time fairly relaxed. Her short hair is just beginning to turn grey. She is in her early forties, and her partner is just a few months older than herself. She arrived a few minutes late for the session. She said that she had hoped for half an hour for herself beforehand, but that a client had been booked in whom she wasn't expecting. Inevitably, she did not have the time and space for herself at that point, since the session started as soon as she arrived. Morag's sentences sometimes tended to shift direction half-way through. This did not appear to involve a total change of subject, but there was often some rephrasing in mid-sentence of what she wanted to say. Some words were then difficult to catch. There has been some slight tidying up of this in the account to retain the sense of her sentences, but has been kept in part to show more exactly the effect of this rapid movement from one thought to another.

Much of the time in the first part of the session, Morag spoke fluently and with little obvious feeling, except momentarily when she spoke of growing old with her partner. The second part of the session flowed less easily, and some of the silences were broken by the male therapist. These interventions are included in the text. These are included where they involved taking Morag back to former phrases she had used rather than taking up the immediate last few words. The second part of the session contained many more pauses, and much more hesitancy over choice of words. There was more evident feeling, although also some sense of her imposing self-control and looking for intelligent explanations.

The family situation is that I live with a partner – we're not married – we have a five-year-old daughter. He has two children, thirteen and fifteen, and (this is a bit of the background) . . . I work . . . I've got two jobs really. I'm an accountant. I have my own private business, which I started when I had my daughter, and I found that people weren't all that willing to be fairly flexible about employment, which I would like; and the second thing that I do is that I have a mobile catering business, doing business lunches, which employs about fifteen single-parent staff. It really was . . . I started that because there seemed to be a gap in the market, that could be filled by people with similar child-care problems to myself.

I suppose there are two areas I'd like help with. The first area is when . . . although I get on quite well with the stepchildren and they come to me at the weekend, although they are at boarding school . . . they tend during term time to be . . . one comes one weekend and the other another weekend. I find that I feel very aggressive when they walk in and it takes me a while, and it seems to take them . . . it's almost . . . it isn't till the end of the weekend that we're used to living with each other again.

Trying to analyse why this is, I feel in a way that we have not exactly a peaceful home, but quite . . . when there's only the three of us there, you get used to doing certain things, and they can walk in on Friday, and they're immediately there, and for some reason wherever you are that's where they want to be, so you suddenly feel very crowded. But not only that, they are at the age where they are fairly sure about what they want and what they don't want. The boy, who's the older one – fifteen – is particularly . . . I find him particularly selfish. He will only do whatever he wants to do. Now I know this is a problem of all children, and probably if they were my own children I would probably make allowances and excuses, but I find that they walk in and they just take. They don't help with anything unless you ask them to do so. The last time they made us a cup of tea was when they were about eight years old.

They just don't do anything. I feel they can sense I'm aggressive when they walk in. I know I shouldn't be. [*Morag is not at all angry as she says all this. She is quite calm.*] I should be able to be cool and think that it doesn't matter. If ever you ask them to do anything, it's 'I'm busy doing something else', or 'wait a minute' or whatever, and then it's passed. I don't know whether I should be getting them to understand that I feel that as a family everybody should have to do their bit. I don't know whether it's partly because . . . one other thing connected with it, and it's something that I have been totally – not exactly puzzled by, because I think it's almost a biological thing – is that whenever James talks about his ex-wife, she's . . . I suppose I feel she's pretty hopeless. She works for a couple of hours a week, and her father's firm pays an extortionate amount for the amount that she does. But she can never . . . James has to do the rushing around for the children. James always has to go and get them from school, pick them up from school, and I know that she only has . . . her name only has to be mentioned and I can feel myself inside sort of knotting up. And it doesn't matter what she does or anything. I just feel cross about it [*she laughs*].

She's just so hopeless. But maybe it's to do with who I'm now living with . . . she actually left James, so it wasn't any question that I should feel any grudge towards her or she should feel anything towards me at all. We did I actually – looked after the children for two years. I suppose I feel that my anger to her, if you like, I can contain. Not contain, but it doesn't affect my life that often, because she isn't mentioned that often, but the children (this is a bit of background) did come and live with us for two years. She suddenly said that she couldn't cope with them . . . first of all she wanted to go to college, she felt that she had looked after them for so long; then she decided that she needed a bit of mental help . . . and then, for me who is a very practical person, somebody that just gets on with things, I really feel that she's just so . . . not exactly laid back, but that she doesn't know what she's doing or whatever. And it annoys me the effect that it has on the children, because she can upset the children, because if she gets upset she tends to transmit it to Debbie, who's particularly vulnerable, and then Debbie feels she's got to look after her. I suppose I feel she shouldn't be doing that. She should be looking at her own life and not worrying about her mother's.

I feel that – I'm probably selfish – but I feel that she's a very selfish person. She doesn't do anything if it doesn't suit her to do it. As soon as you ask her to do something which she doesn't want to do, she says she can't possibly do that, she can't possibly handle it. To give you an idea, Debbie went to boarding school. She was quite keen to go to boarding school to begin with, but when she was there she found she was homesick, so we talked about her coming back. I know she couldn't handle Debbie full time if she was at home. Sooner or later she would get fed up with her and fed up with the responsibility for her. I suppose Paula is a bit like somebody who has never grown up. She hasn't reached . . . she's a similar age to her children, she's about fifteen. She liked them when they were small, because they were in a sort of way dolls. But going back to this boarding thing – then she'd say to Debbie, 'Look, I think you could come and live with me', and I get really cross because I know that she'd know in her heart of hearts, and we knew, that she wouldn't be able to cope with it. So why does she lead the child on? And let her suggest that she could live with her mum, when it wouldn't actually happen? That makes me a bit cross.

The second thing that I perhaps wanted to talk about is . . . I'd like to understand why I enjoy doing things. I enjoy challenges. I really like doing up Victorian houses. I've never lived in anything long enough to have to redecorate. I've always been on the move. To relax, I either have to read a book, and get totally immersed in that, and then nobody can talk to me then, or I have to be doing something else. I can go on a different course, and I find that totally relaxing because I'm doing something totally different. Whereas I think possibly for James, and for the people I have lived with – I suppose I've lived with people for a period of six or seven years – I think they find it very exhausting trying to keep up with me, in that I find it . . . not exactly boring. I enjoy my life and what I do, I enjoy my two jobs and meeting a lot of people; you know you get some interesting problems. And the catering business – he was not very keen on me to set it up because he felt it would take a lot of time away from him, but the idea's been a big challenge. It's only coming up to two years old. I got it going. I got the capital and equipment for it. I set it up. It's now ticking over. It's now getting a very good reputation; and I want to do something else! I want to know really – I suppose I find the weekends not exactly boring, but I don't like cleaning and hoovering and washing up. I do them because I have to, and I feel that James wants me to be in the house, to be there because his children are there, and the family's there. He's quite happy to go off and play rugby on Sunday but he likes me being there being the mother-hen. I just . . . I get quite cross, that he keeps trying to push me into the traditional role. He'll say, 'I cooked a meal for you'; and I say, 'That's very kind, don't you cook it for everybody?'; or 'I put the dishwasher on for you' and it . . . I suppose in my professional life, I don't feel I've got on as far as I could have done had I been a man, because I had to work twice as hard as everybody else to get where I got, and it's . . . I don't know, I suppose I need to find . . . I feel OK always wanting to do something, but it does seem to cause quite a lot of conflict in my life. I feel, 'Is it right that I should always be wanting something new to go at, some new challenge? Should I just be accepting the way I am?'

I get very frustrated by, for example, James, who works very hard during the week – he's a managing director in a family company . . . the chairman is his ex-father-in-law, so it's a bit of a difficult situation. He was a photographer by training, and he was good at it – he actually won prizes – but he found it couldn't pay as well as he needed it to, teaching it and that sort of thing, and so it's a bit of a conflict for him. He's not really . . . I know other people in business who relish things, enjoy them, the cut and thrust of business, enjoy the challenge of making something. I enjoy that, but I think he struggles. I suppose I feel frustrated – if he doesn't enjoy his job, he should do something else. One only gets one life. But because he works fairly hard at that, he tends to flop at the weekend, and just potter and do the garden.

I get itchy, I want to do something new. Because everything's arranged jointly I can't do it without him. I have to drag him with me; but at the same time it is thrown at me from time to time that I'm not normal, that most people don't quite have the energy or the need to do things the whole time. It results in a conflict, especially at weekends, when I want to get up and do something, or go out and see something, and he doesn't. If I lived on my own I would probably not worry about it, but some bit of me says that . . . I was married for a while, and then I lived with two people, for about six or seven years each, and I suppose each one of them has ended up saying, 'It was an interesting experience, but I'm glad it's over'. [*Morag laughs*.] The frightening feeling is, should I try and calm down, should I try not to do quite so much, for I suppose the happiness of the relationship? When you don't have children in-volved it's easier to take up and leave, but I feel that having a child is more of a commitment than actually marrying somebody, be-cause you never actually get away from that person, that person is always part of your life, because of the child. I'm fairly determined that I want this relationship to stay, and you know, to grow old together. [*At this point, Morag's eyes water and she goes quiet.*]

He's often said that he's never really been looked after by some-one, by anybody. His father spent a lot of time out. His mother was a fairly weak person and I think needed quite a lot of support. And he feels that his wife needed support as well; I think that's partly what attracted him . . . what in me attracted him, was the fact that I was fairly independent and didn't need looking after. It's almost in a sense what he's trying to change now. Having got an independ-ent person, he's not quite sure whether he really does want an independent person. He frequently says that he would like to be looked after, that I don't really take enough care of them. I suppose I feel it's a two-way thing. I cook him most of the meals; occasion-ally, I say, 'Would you cook because I want to do some work?' He wants me to change roles, if you like, to be the nurturing mother-hen at the weekend, which doesn't lie easily on me.

I do more with his children than he does. When he comes home in the evening and has a meal, he wants to watch television because he wants to switch off, because unless his brain switches off by the time he goes to sleep he won't be able to sleep. And at the weekends he can spend Saturday morning out, but then he can spend most of Sunday watching the television, which to me is just a total waste of time. His idea of entertaining the children is to watch the television with them. Whereas I do take them ice-skating, or take them out and suggest things, or drag the whole family out somewhere. I'm just not that sort of person.

One thing I haven't mentioned, James is fanatically tidy. Paula kept the house tidy, but she drank quite a lot. The children wouldn't be allowed to untidy the house so the house was tidy for James. He says I'm fanatically untidy, but I don't think I am. Most people who walk into our house think how tidy it is. He's got a darkroom, and he can't start working in it until he's tidied everything away, until everything's just so, which is a bit surprising for someone who's basically artistic, I would have thought. And he does that at home. When he's anxious about anything he starts tidying, slamming doors, and making huffing and puffing sounds, which is all meant to make me feel guilty about the fact that I haven't kept it . . . for me it's more important . . . we have an interesting house, it's open-plan and it's great fun. But it does mean that you can see everything; but to me a house is to be lived in, it's more important that somebody should feel welcome and should feel that they can sit down and put the bag anywhere, than feel they've got to put the bag by the front door, sit in the right place, and that sort of thing.

In those terms, Paula probably did look after him. Yet he says that several times that she didn't look after the children, and he would have to come home and sort them out. It's a little bit difficult to get to the truth of what actually did happen. I know he would have stuck with the marriage – because he loved her and loved the children, and it was an uncomfortable wrench for them suddenly to be taken away from him. He blames Paula having seen a counsellor just before their marriage broke up. He says that the counsellor persuaded her that the marriage was at an end.

[*There is a short silence. The therapist asks her what she was thinking.*]

It flashed through my mind that I was supposed to keep talking, and what should I talk about, and should I go on to something different? [*The therapist says that she can go on to something different if she wants to, although he also says he wonders about her saying that he would not have wanted the marriage to end, and what that means to her when Paula's name is mentioned.*]

It doesn't particularly worry me, because I don't think he'd ever . . . No, it doesn't worry me. I don't think he would go back to live with her. He lived on his own for a while. She hurt him immensely. I don't think he'll ever get over that. One of the things he says to me if we've had an argument, and I've walked away, and when he's in the process of – well not of making up, but that sort of thing – he'll say, 'You won't ever leave me, will you?' I realized from the start of our relationship that I would probably have to be the prime mover if we had to split up. Occasionally, I say to him, 'Look I just cannot cope with being criticized'. We got to the stage where he'd come in and he'd criticize the house for being untidy. Well, he wouldn't come in, he'd criticize just before we go to bed at night, which is obviously when you're at your weakest, and lowest. And he'd almost pick a fight. And it got to the point when I'd say, 'I'm not going to put up with these criticisms any more. I do lots of things for you. I make sure the whole house runs OK. I do the washing, the ironing' – we have some help but he usually throws that back at me that 'I organized the help'. He . . . I thought that the only thing that would actually split us up would be if he criticized me so much that I couldn't cope with arguments at night. I've learned to cope with it a bit more, in that I actually walk away, and say I'm going to sleep downstairs or whatever. I have learned to walk away. Usually in the morning he's fairly repentant. Every time we have an argument, he tends to be fairly repentant and sends me flowers or something like this.

It may be – well, I suppose it's two things. He finds he can't live in a place that's untidy; and I'm not prepared to spend every hour tidying up, especially with a five-year-old. Maybe it's slightly different in that I've taken the top of the house – that's my and my daughter's sort of den. It can be a mess, and he never comes in there and it doesn't matter. And that eases the situation. He doesn't actually have to walk into where my daughter's been playing – *our* daughter's been playing. In a sense when I say '*my* daughter', it *is* my daughter because he didn't actually . . . he wasn't all that keen to have another child. He'd had two and had quite a lot of problems with them. But it's one of the things that I made quite clear when we got together, that I did want a child. If you like, it was part of the package. And he, after soul-searching, accepted that. But I guess that I can't complain that he's not all that wonderful with Jessica, because he's not really very good with the rest of his children.

He does very little with . . . I mean she's not untidy, she's untidy in her room. I say things like, 'You know, you're the tidy one, you should be showing her how to tidy', but it's always pushed back on to me. He doesn't . . . she can have holidays like she's had, and he'll say he'll see her at weekends and go on holiday with her. And that sounds a bit cold and clinical, but I think he feels he's being as much of a father as he really should be. I feel that he gets so stressed up with his work, that it makes the rest of his life . . . he gets stressed up at home. And I feel that we're suffering because he's basically in a job that he's not really that suited to, but determination won't let him drop it. Pride and self-esteem won't let him drop it. I'd like him . . . if he's not happy doing it.

I think he feels jealous of my work. When I set up the catering business it was: 'You'll split the family by doing this. You'll split us up'. He didn't say 'us' . . . always said 'the family'. You know: 'the family will suffer'. But I think in fact that he meant *he* would suffer. There wouldn't be quite so much time to give him. That's part of the trouble. I'm doing a job that I enjoy, that I like. And he's not. All I can do is say to him, 'Well, you leave and do what you'd like, and then everyone would be a lot happier'. But then maybe they wouldn't. Maybe I shouldn't suggest that to people because some people can't cope with . . . if you like, their own . . . if they've got *carte blanche* to do what they want, they can't think what they do want. [*She pauses.*] Yes, it's a problem.

[*There is another pause, and the therapist wants to get back more obviously to her. He refers to what she said earlier about other relationships, and the relief for her partners at the ending. He wonders how she was affected by those relationships and the end of those relationships. Hesitantly at first, Morag responded.*]

I tend to look forward rather than back. I got married when I was about twenty-one, and we lived together for a couple of years at college, and he was also an accountant. He also did very little at the weekend, although we were doing a place up. Then I felt I'd got the wrong person, that we weren't really compatible. In fact he's more or less much the same as James: worked very hard at work, but he didn't want to do anything at weekends. He also metaphorically used to pat me on the head. I always used to think that he'd never think that I was as good an accountant as he was, whereas in fact I definitely am. [*She laughs at this.*] And he also wanted children at that stage and I knew that if I had children at that stage, my career – I'd be totally swamped.

The relationship probably that I do look back on quite a lot is the relationship before James. Probably. I lived with somebody that I had hoped to get married to and I had hoped to have children with and all the rest of it. And I was let down. I found he was having another affair with somebody else while he was living with me. Obviously, that involved a certain amount of lying. He had his own accountancy firm. He was great fun to be with. We got on very well business-wise. When I meet him now we do talk a lot, but I suppose I decided that I couldn't live with somebody if I didn't know whether they were telling the truth or not. And that relationship came to a head because I accused him of having an affair. And we decided that, as we happened to have another house we were re-doing at the time, we should live apart for a while. And we said we would work on the house and see each other at weekends. And at that point, I had said . . . it came out in conversation that he was never going to marry *me*; and I think I felt about rock-bottom then. I went away and thought about it, and thought, 'If he's going to do this I'm not going to sit at home waiting for him. I'm going to go out and meet other people, swimming' – that's where I met James, swimming. And I did meet James and the other chap – whose name is Carl – then said, 'If you like I'm prepared to forget that you've gone out with this other chap. I'll forgive you for going out with each other'. And I said, 'Hey! Hang on a sec. You've brought this on yourself. I'm not sure I don't want to see James again. I would like to see him some more'. And I think it was only at that stage that Carl realized that there was actually a fear of losing me. I think he thought I was so much in love with him, which I was, that he could more or less do anything, and I'd come back.

And then I started going out with James. And I'm not quite sure which one of them it was, but one of them said, 'Look this is not good. We don't want you going out with two people at once'; and so I had to make a decision fairly early on, which one to . . . probably before I was ready . . . probably in a sense before I knew a lot about James. But I think even then I had the feeling that it was James I could totally depend on, and that he would never leave me; whereas I think with Carl I still felt that if I'd gone back it would have been a merry dance that he led me. Yes, he was more sociable; you know, we liked inviting people for a meal and things like this. We had our work in common, though we fought about our house that we lived in . . . although I think that's inevitable when you get two people doing the same . . . whereas James and I tend to agree on the houses that we go for. But I suppose occasionally I look back with regret at that, because he . . . we had many things in common in a sense, but on the other hand he wasn't . . . you know, I could see that it would also be a problem to me. [*She pauses.*]

We were doing this house up at the weekend, and he was very sociable. I think he needed to socialize, because he wanted to get other work and he needed contacts. But he enjoyed socializing. So there was always something, sometimes almost too much going on at weekends. James is active in that he'll mow the lawn, and if anything needs mending he'll mend it, and that sort of thing. Carl would put as many ideas into the relationship as I would. It was an interesting time.

James, especially about my work, he's very encouraging. He thinks I'm talented and he'll praise me to other people. It's just where it comes in conflict with him that there's a problem.

[*There is another pause, as if Morag has come to the end of what she*

*wants to say for the time being. The therapist reminds her that earlier she
had said she would like to analyse what this is all about. He asks her
what ideas she has about it.*]
 [*She spends a short time thinking.*] I think that in terms of my work,
obviously James feels a certain amount of jealousy, though I don't
know what to do about that. The other thing is that James never
wants to talk about my work, which I find quite a strain, being on
my own. I work with people on the catering side – I've got someone
in charge, so I talk about the business problems with her. But as far
as accountancy goes, I don't have anybody that I can actually talk . . .
about . . . in terms of . . . maybe I'm being perhaps unfair to James
in the . . . at the back of my mind comparing it to when I used to
live with Carl, but I don't . . . I don't suppose . . . maybe that's there
in my subconscious, but I very rarely think about Carl unless it's
in terms of a work problem I've got. I'll still ring him up and say,
'I can't . . . This and this has happened with this client. What do
you recommend that I do?' But I only see him . . . we go out for an
annual drink just once a year. [*She pauses.*] But maybe that is affecting me, my life without him. I don't really know.
 [*Morag pauses again. She is now speaking very slowly. The therapist
pushes her gently on this last remark, but also says he is not sure she
wants to follow it through.*]
 I suppose the situation with Carl was quite painful, and still is a
bit painful. In those terms I guess it's likely to be important. [*She
pauses again.*] I guess it's like anything. I think when things don't go
well, you start thinking that the grass is greener elsewhere. And I
think when you're happy and things are active, you don't consider
things that don't go very well . . .
 [*She pauses yet again. The therapist says, 'There are still things about
the relationship with Carl that you find yourself missing?'*]
 Yes, I miss the working relationship, and being able to talk business to him. I can't with James, no matter whether it's his business
we're talking about, or my business, or something that's connected.
I always feel that James goes off on a total red herring. I get frustrated that we're not getting to the nub of the problem. And I never
did . . . it was always one thing that we could always have been very
good business partners . . . I suppose actually what comes back to me
about putting down . . . when Carl was very unhappy in his particular firm . . . the other managers . . . he had a meeting with them . . . the
other managers in his firm suggested that I might join them. I think
he thought he was the only young one, and didn't have any support
and they felt he needed somebody around that would be quite
good. And Carl dismissed it, I think probably because he thought we
were a bit unsettled at the time and he didn't obviously want to get

into a permanent situation with somebody that might not be . . . but I suppose that hurt quite a lot, because I would have been good for the business, because I'm quite a practical person, and the person he eventually took on was a very good accountant but totally hopeless in terms of her organization and . . . she's only interested in figures and not in the whole of the approach. [*There is a short silence.*]

The trouble is, I suppose . . . maybe I should do a bit of exorcism on the Carl time. I suppose by definition . . . it really would be . . . [*she hesitates*] . . . the feelings you had for him [*Morag's voice cracks and she looks rather upset*] so that it would let you go on and do something else. [*She is silent, and then speaks quietly.*] But how do you do that? I'm not quite sure.

I'm just thinking that this has taken a totally different turn. I actually don't think about him. [*Again she is quiet.*] I'm always very conscious, very careful, if I say that I've been talking to Carl to James . . . how I actually say that I have . . . because I suppose that I can sense that he probably senses that there is something that he might be worried about.

[*Again at this point her voice cracks. She appears to have become quite sad. She wipes her eyes. The therapist breaks the short silence by observing that she also looked a little sad when she talked about wanting to grow old with James. Morag is still lost for words, and begins to talk very slowly.*]

I think . . . yes . . . perhaps it's what everybody strives for, a relationship that will last, that . . . that, will not . . . I think that . . . I do . . . I definitely do . . . I mean I set out . . . I suppose the time I met Carl I wanted a relationship that was going to last. There's so much hurt involved when you do split up with somebody. Not so much with my husband, but the person that I left to get together with Carl, I could see that I'd hurt him an awful lot . . . and I think you want to . . . you don't want so much pain involved. In a sense it's daft, because I'm not . . . I can sense you're thinking, 'Ah, something about the pain involved when she left Carl or when Carl left'. But . . . yes, there was a lot of hurt . . . but I suppose I didn't feel guilty about that hurt, because I felt that what happened when I left with James . . . Carl went through a very bad period and wanted me to come back and was generally very depressed for several months. He made our friends' lives fairly miserable by going round and pouring out his heart evening after evening. So in a sense at the end of the day it was me who decided that I was going to live with James, and not get involved with . . . not give Carl another chance, provided that he . . . I suppose in terms of this growing old together, I could see that it wouldn't happen, that I wouldn't be with Carl in ten years' time. So I didn't feel very guilty about the pain that he was suffering, because I thought he very much brought it upon himself. But I did feel that about the previous chap. I think you do . . . maybe it's a romantic ideal that one wants to settle down and . . . just have somebody you feel comfortable with and you want to do things with and you . . .

I think that something that appealed to me about James to start off with was that he always appeared very calm. He doesn't appear very calm now . . . [*She laughs.*] Perhaps that's why . . . I know there's the link of Jessica, but I do feel that the relationship we've got, that it will work, that we will stay together. But it's just a question of how you can perhaps come to . . . either come to terms with it and work it. I suppose for me it's that I have to see a way forward. If I think about a problem, I try and think about a course of action. Once I've decided on that course of action I follow that through, and OK – maybe you have to review that and go a different way – but I'd like to feel I'm improving the situation, and that I'm not making life very difficult for James. And OK, although he doesn't want me to leave, I'm actually causing him a few problems, making his life more . . . I'd like to feel I make his life happy. But at the moment I tend to feel that he's not very happy. I probably am responsible for it in some way. I suppose I don't feel I'm the underlying reason, but maybe that's me not accepting that I feel responsible. Maybe I'm wanting him to change his job so that he's happy or whatever as a sop for me saying 'It's not really me that's making you feel unhappy'.

The problem is that one would like to be able to change oneself to suit someone else. But at the end of the day you can't do that. I think I've done that through different relationships. I've tried to be somebody that I'm not, and so I have a feeling that they've either got to accept you as you are, or they've not, and they've got to make that decision. And they've not got to try and criticize the whole time.

One thing that I feel I should . . . mention it, because it may have a bearing . . . I don't think that it affected me as much as it affected James, but when I first got pregnant I was ill, and it was likely I might have a handicapped child; and I decided to terminate the pregnancy because I felt that it just would have totally have affected my life in a way that I didn't want it affected; that it would be all the worst things about having a child. I think James felt . . . he was also at the birth of Jessica, and I know he found it very difficult to be there. His wife had a lot of pain, particularly with the second child, and I think he probably felt that I put him through two lots of pain, one with the termination and one with Jessica. And he does occasionally bring this up from time to time . . . I'm not sure . . . I suppose I feel I've accepted it, or I accepted it when it happened. If you like, the daughter that I've got fills the space and everything, and so I don't feel guilty about it. But James does occasionally . . . I would probably have liked another child, but I think James didn't really want . . . it was a bit of protest for him to accept the one in the first place, and now I'm probably getting a bit too old and my daughter's nearly six now.

3

THE READER'S
RESPONSE

Before reading further, the reader is given space to record a personal response to the client, and to similar questions which the six therapists were asked to address.

What does this client make you feel?

How might you use what you feel in understanding and working with this client?

What more do you want to know? Is there any information which is crucial at this stage?

Thus far, how do you understand this client and the material the client has presented?

What indications are there so far in this client that lead you to feel that you could work with her?

What contraindications are there?

What, if any, will be your focus?

What will be your method, as related to this client?

What difficulties do you anticipate you might encounter?

What in your view might be a favourable outcome for this client?

ROXANE AGNEW

4

FOCUSED EXPRESSIVE
PSYCHOTHERAPY

The therapist

My early training as a clinical psychologist was heavily biased towards cognitive behavioural approaches. I liked the collaborative emphasis in these methods and I felt contained and supported by the structured framework that lent confidence and implied validity. I am particularly drawn to the reconstruction of fundamental assumptions and still practise cognitive behavioural therapy with clients. However, at times the approach felt superficial, inadequate and almost a denial of the reality of a client's emotion: like one woman's grief after losing her husband and son in the same year, or another's experience of multiple sexual abuse. Later, I valued the insights into the therapeutic relationship and therapeutic process I gained from a study of Hobson's conversational model (Hobson 1985); but I also felt stilted and constrained, in a vacuum where feelings were a by-product and therapy an intellectual exercise.

Looking back, I was struggling with stereotypical assumptions about the role of emotion in personal experience and therapeutic change. Crudely, these assumptions involved:

- regarding 'negative' emotions as undesirable, as hindrances to development, which moved the person to act in irrational or disorganized ways;
- regarding emotions as a lower, primitive level of functioning, surpassed by cognitions, such that cognitive processes precede and overpower their affective counterparts;
- regarding therapeutic efforts as attempts to regulate emotion, with attention being directed at the emotion only in the service of accessing cognitions.

Focused Expressive Psychotherapy (FEP), developed by Roger Daldrup in Tucson, Arizona, validated my personal beliefs by offering a different framework for understanding emotion. Briefly, the approach assumes that:

- No feeling is 'good' or 'bad', but (more akin to breathing) simply 'is'.
- The experience of emotion is natural and valid.
- Strategies for suppressing or controlling emotion have often developed as adaptive responses to help the person grow up, to fit others' expectations and/or to survive traumatic experiences. However, these early decisions about dealing with emotional events often carry through to adult life in a way that is no longer appropriate or healthy.
- Emotions are intricately bound up with perception, learning and memory; emotional and cognitive development and behaviour are integrally related. I am continuing to learn to interweave emotional experience with its significance or meaning (to relate it to cognitive structures); and I have supplemented FEP in this regard through Gestalt training with David Engle and Marj Holiman from Arizona.
- In therapy, accessing emotion can direct attention, is frequently associated with significant psychological change and is crucial in the ongoing development of a sense of self (and self in relation to others).

My discovery of FEP, which matches that of many of the clients and therapists I have worked with since, has felt like 'coming home'. I also want to acknowledge that, in addition to being forever indebted to Roger Daldrup, David Engle and Marj Holiman, I continue to benefit and learn from the application of FEP principles in my personal relationship with Bryn Davies, and in my clinical practice with Gary Burton.

Further information requested

When working in FEP, I pay attention to the process (how her story is told) as well as to the content of Morag's answers. To give a sense of this, I include indices of her non-verbal behaviour (such as hesitations), signs of affect, or ways in which she discounts emotions (non-verbally by laughter, or verbally in phrases such as 'sort of').

First, I asked Morag about how she normally expressed sadness, fear and anger:

[Sadness]: I possibly get angry if someone hurts me. I probably attack back. Um . . . ; I think I've er . . . sunk fairly low and then decided . . . that enough was enough and to try to get out and busy myself with something else.

[Fear]: I try to do the sensible thing . . . and rationalize.

[Anger]: Er . . . if . . . I do . . . er . . . I think that I probably er . . . might store up things for a short time, but I . . . you know, I do occasionally er . . . blow and er . . . usually if . . . the person attacks me again . . . then . . . [*little laugh*] my defence is 'well, you know, while we're talking about it . . .' [*laughs*] . . . if I'm really totally fed up . . . I'll . . . er . . . have a moan I suppose, [*laughs*], but that's not really angry.

I then explained that her answers were probably influenced by rules or scripts she adopted while living with significant people in her life, and asked how Morag's parents expressed emotions and appreciation of her.
Take my father first: I don't think I've ever seen him express any sadness *ever* . . . He was definitely one of the stiff upper-lip type of variety . . . [Appreciation of me?]: Um . . . I don't think he . . . ever did really [*little laugh*]. Er . . . I mean, he . . . er . . . my sister used to be his sort of favourite, and then because she wasn't all that bright, and I, achieved well at school . . . his attention went from her more toward me . . . um . . . But I can't remember him ever saying, 'Well done!'

[My mother]: Yes, well, sadness, she'll burst into tears or be upset. She's more demonstrative. [Anger]: She probably tends to . . . deal with anger in a hurt sort of way. She does er . . . lash out, if er . . . she's been hurt, but she also . . . perceives hurt where I don't think it's really intended. [Fear]: She's quite fearful about what people think of her . . . unwarranted, and she tends to sort of . . . shrink back, and then . . . mildly attack, I suppose, but as a defence.

[Later in the interview]: She was brought up with an ethic that you should do anything you can to help anybody else. She actually doesn't feel she's doing well unless she's helping somebody. And I admire her tremendously for that . . . I guess it must have come from her . . . I really should try . . . I would feel happier if I was doing more for other people.

What conclusions did you reach about expressing feelings when you were a little girl?
If . . . I . . . had a bit of a moan [*laughs*], my mother would say, 'Oh, go away' [*laughs*], 'get on with it' . . . I distinctly

remember her saying 'Don't tell tales to me' . . . and 'Life is not fair'.

I suggested that Morag might have a script, about trying to be someone she wasn't, to please someone.
Very true with Carl . . . I was very deeply attached to him, but he put me on a pedestal. I definitely remember thinking, 'This is no good, I'm trying to be somebody I'm not. I just want to be myself, and I want somebody that wants me for myself'. That was an important changeover point.

I asked her about the script that she shouldn't take time and space for herself.
In my heart of hearts I knew, to get a pat on the back . . . I'd got to do well at something, and because of that I . . . actually achieve . . . If somebody criticizes me it means I'm not doing very well. And that's why it hurts.

In extending the question about rules adopted in living with significant people, Morag referred to both James and her ex-husband. When thinking of James, Morag recognized 'he will shout, hgh! He tidies up, and bangs doors [*laughs*] . . . I always know that something's wrong . . . er . . . and then he explodes'. Morag was aware of James's fear that she might leave him. She contrasted her relationship with him to other partners: 'James is the only one . . . where we can have an argument . . . and I think that's perhaps a good thing . . . whereas [others] didn't express too much one way or the other and that's why they didn't survive'.
When thinking of her ex-husband, Morag talked mostly of his lack of appreciation of her: 'He was always putting me down . . . And I guess I felt . . . a bit trapped [into having kids]. I don't think he expressed too much sort of appreciation'.

I asked Morag about internal struggles, including the battle between the part that is busy and solves problems, and the part that gets worn out. I asked her to give a voice to the second part:
[*Speaks quietly, slowly and reflectively.*] I feel tired . . . I guess life was very simple when you just had yourself . . . you have all these responsibilities and . . . I guess I'm my own worst enemy . . . by erecting more problems like the second business I've started up . . .' [*Another silence.*] [Later in the interview]: I do get . . . fed up, that it's . . . all landed on me [*sigh*].

I explained that rules about suppressing feelings can create 'unfinished business' (unresolved feelings about past or current relationships). I asked

*Morag about her relationships with several people and to pay attention to
her body and emotions. I also asked whether she would be willing to work
on these feelings and what predictions she made as she anticipated that
work. After specific questions (in brackets) about her feelings towards
James, Morag replied:*

[When he rushes around for *his* [her emphasis] children]: I
suppose I get fed up . . . maybe I'm jealous of him . . . I can
feel a certain sort of anger, well yes, sort of tightening in my
chest.

[When he talks about Paula]: 'Oh . . . I get yes . . . that's
definite, Paula only has to be mentioned and I . . . feel really
'aagh!' . . . that tends to be in my jaw when I feel like
screaming [*laughs*].

[When he expects you to be the traditional wife]: I
suppose I tend to sigh a bit, like that [*sighs and laughs*] . . . I
feel guilty that I'm not taking enough care of him . . . not
living up to what I should be as a partner.

[When he doesn't enjoy his job]: Frustration . . . again . . .
sigh a bit . . . he should do something about it [*laughs*] . . . I
suppose I just feel a bit drained.

[Criticizes you for being untidy]: Cross . . . he's probably
right. [*Pauses.*] I don't know what I feel [*laughs*] . . . I feel I do
a lot . . .

[When he doesn't act as the father]: Feel sad . . . sigh a bit.

[When he goes off on red herrings]: Frustrated . . . getting
tense [*aagh, sigh*].

[Thinking about growing old together]: I want to . . . feel
happy by him . . .

*Morag was willing to make a commitment to work on her feelings towards
James ('Yes, sure') but anticipated some anxieties in doing so:*

I'd be wary of telling James too much about . . . [*pauses*] . . .
the trouble is every time I say something I think . . . er . . . I
don't want to hurt him . . . he . . . can be hurt quite easily . . .
but the second thing is that he'd probably attack me back
anyway. And so I end up feeling hurt anyway, so, um, I'm
not entirely sure [*laughs*] whether it would be . . . productive
. . . but if it led me to a greater understanding so that I
could . . . react differently and therefore bring more peace . . .
that would be a good thing.

Feelings towards Carl

My overwhelming feeling is hurt. [*Thinks for a while.*] It
brings me close to tears . . . [*pauses*] . . . I feel sad, because I

feel we were very well suited and he threw it away [*upset, sighs and pauses*] ... He made up this fantasy about what I was like ... and, er ... I didn't live up to it [*upset, talking quietly*] ... if I feel angry at all it's just that ... he threw it away. That he had an affair ... Um ... [*Voice resumes strength.*] And ... that he, after I got together with James ... suggested we have an affair ...

[Morag remembers that one of Carl's partners suggested that she join the firm, and Carl 'rejected it out of hand'. She continues]: He didn't want me to be involved ... less sure about the relationship than I was; but secondly, he may have thought that I wasn't, you know, that I wasn't good enough.

I asked whether Morag wanted to work on feelings towards Carl, and predictions about that work.
Well, I obviously feel very sad whenever I think about Carl [*upset*]. Yes, I would like to work on it, because I think it is something ... that ... does affect me [*pause*]. That probably is, er ... the most worrying of any, because, um ... er ... I find it difficult to cope with getting upset. Angry, I don't mind [*laughs*]. I can cope with it. But, upset, I find more difficult. I still find ... I'm very attracted towards him ... [*her voice breaks*] ... so yes, I would like to work on it ... It feels that it would be painful, and one doesn't usually willingly give oneself to pain [*laughs*]. (I am) hopeful of the eventual outcome – it'll be worth it.

I asked Morag about her termination of pregnancy and she was clear that it was not a problem area. I asked about her relationship with James's children, and she readily identified feelings of being 'cross' with some 'hope' and optimism that she could feel 'less aggressive towards them'.

Towards the end of the interview, I asked Morag about her feelings towards Paula, paying particular attention to physical responses.
Anger, frustration, mainly ... definitely tension. Probably at the back of my throat [*points*]; I feel very ugh!, sort of knotted just at the mention of her name ...

Can you list some of the things you feel specifically hurt or angry about?
[*Sighs deeply, pauses, then speaks quite quickly*]: I get angry that she's so hopeless ... And I think it is ... a selfish device. I think she's a very self-centred person and she doesn't really care who she hurts. She's very manipulative and especially

good with words. She can turn any comment into an attack . . . very good at deflecting any implied criticism . . . It annoys me that she hurts her children, um . . .

Lastly, I asked Morag about her reactions to the questions that I had asked.
I find it interesting, um . . . the body is giving you physical cues about your mental state and . . . it's . . . useful because it does pin-point . . . as a barometer of your strength of feelings about something, or alternatively as a warning system, but, you know there's something there that maybe you should look at a bit more.

Assessment

In FEP, the therapist relies on process diagnosis – a description of the client's current processes, rather than a categorization. Rather than diagnosing stable traits, an FEP therapist examines and responds to what the client is doing (what she exhibits and how she tells her story) and her feeling in the present (since emotions are a means to orient a person in their interaction with the world). Process diagnosis leads to the identification of in-session 'markers' – issues on which I can invite Morag to focus, and to which I can respond with specific interventions (such as the creation of an 'experiment'). In FEP, these markers are typically concerned with unfinished business.

Because therapists are guided by the client's description of what emerges for him or her, they avoid interpretations. However, the requirements of this project (with reliance on verbal transcript) lead me to interpret in a way which I would not normally do. Given the limitations (since I do not have access to detailed information on Morag's processing style, or her immediate reactions to comments), I am speculating that FEP could serve Morag in the following ways.

Focused Expressive Psychotherapy is an approach specifically designed to help people who suppress or over-control their emotions. First, there is evidence that Morag over-controls her feelings and that she is aware of doing so. She reports expressing hurt indirectly, by retaliating (masking upset with anger), or by 'sinking fairly low' and then 'busying' herself to distract herself from her sadness. She describes trying to rationalize fear away. She tends to 'leak' anger indirectly, or by 'moaning', and within the sessions I am aware that Morag often laughs off an emotion that she is experiencing and hesitates when expressing a feeling directly. She also uses qualifiers

such as 'sort of' or 'you know' to discount the impact of her statement. The assessor commented that Morag imposed self-control and
looked for intelligent explanations.

My understanding is that her decision to over-control feelings
partly came from scripts she learned as a little girl growing up, as
she reconciled discrepancies between what she felt and what she
observed or was told about feelings. Morag reports never seeing her
father express sadness, and describes him as 'the stiff upper-lip variety'. I am struck by her acknowledgement that he did not show
direct appreciation of her. She clearly links her achievements at
school with gaining more of his attention.

I guess her mother also had an important influence on the way
Morag controls feelings. She sees in her mother a similar tendency
to 'attack' if hurt as a defence. In addition, Morag clearly remembers
her mother's impatience if she tried to talk about feelings. She also
learned 'the ethic that you should do anything you can to help
anybody'.

In summary, Morag has had little permission to experience or
talk openly about hurt, anger or fear, and instead has emphasized
looking after other people. She continues to suppress emotions to
protect others (including James), and because she is not used to
considering them as valid, healthy reactions, that can be expressed
safely (without fear of 'attack').

In consequence, Morag has 'unfinished business', or unresolved
feelings towards several people in her life that she struggles to control. For example, she would like to 'exorcize' unresolved feelings
about Carl, although she is unsure how to go about it. I think we
could benefit from exploring this unfinished business in safe ways,
focusing on the following relationships:

With James

Morag talks at various stages about feeling cross, frustrated and fed
up with James's behaviour. She reports feeling guilty (which I link
to suppressed resentment) for not taking enough care of him, and
sad that he and their daughter Jessica (and I suspect Morag herself)
are missing out on a closer relationship. However, she is wary of
talking directly about these feelings as she predicts either he will be
hurt, and/or he will attack back, which would hurt her. (At this
stage, I am highlighting unfinished business, rather than acknowledging the strength of her caring relationship with James.)

With Carl

Morag clearly experiences a lot of emotion as she thinks of Carl.
Primarily she is aware of sadness that 'he threw it away', and at

other times she acknowledges anger (that he had an affair, that he suggested an affair with her and that he rejected her as a partner, which hits home about not being 'good enough'). She feels confusion about her current attraction to him, and predicts that it will be hard to cope with acknowledging her upset feelings. (I guess her attraction can be understood in terms of the 'unfinished business' not being completed, and her desire to achieve that before fully investing in another relationship.)

With Paula

Morag is very aware of changes in her body (feelings like screaming, the tightening in her jaw, 'a knot') when she thinks of Paula. She acknowledges her anger indirectly as she talks of Paula's selfishness, manipulation and hurtful behaviour. However, Morag talks in a blaming, externalized way (rather than honestly and directly expressing anger) that I guess she finds unsatisfying.

With her ex-husband

Morag briefly mentions that her ex-husband 'was always putting me down' and that she felt trapped. My hunch is that her feelings towards him may be linked to unfinished business with her father, about having to meet expectations, or feeling unloved just for being herself. She brings an important change to working through her feelings towards her ex-husband (or others) when she was with Carl. She discovered that she thought: 'This is no good. I'm trying to be someone I'm not. I just want to be myself and I want somebody that wants me for myself'.

With James's children

As Morag reports tension, and typically feeling cross, I want to afford her the opportunity to express her feelings about their behaviour directly (in the session). I see a link between her role as a mother and her feelings towards James and Paula that I would like to explore more.

With her father and/or her mother

In addition, Morag may want to work on unfinished business here, in terms of feelings that she harbours from childhood; for example, about her father's lack of appreciation or her mother's dismissal of feelings.

Apart from the unfinished business, I want to explore some internal conflicts that Morag experiences, which we call 'splits'. We might refer to these in various ways:

- as battles or struggles between the part that is always busy achieving and the part that feels tired;
- or between the part that is the responsible mother and the part that is aware of her own needs and feelings;
- or being upset versus coping;
- or the judge versus the part that feels judged.

For example, Morag says: 'I guess I'm my own worst enemy, that I've added . . . creating more problems like the second business'; and precedes this by saying: 'I feel tired . . . I guess life was very simple when you just had yourself'.

She questions in the first session: 'Is it right that I should always be wanting . . . some new challenge? Should I just be accepting the way I am?' Again, she has ambivalent feelings about challenges and achievements, which we could couch in terms of enjoyment versus fatigue, or own needs versus gaining approval. When I ask her about not taking time and space for herself, she says in her heart she knows she wanted 'to get a pat on the back . . . I'd got to do well at something'; and 'if somebody criticizes me it means I'm not doing very well . . . that's why it hurts'. Since she also 'keeps busy' to keep emotions at bay, I feel concern about the pressure she experiences and her difficulty in acknowledging the heart-felt little voice that says, 'I feel tired'.

In summary, and extending FEP (which primarily focuses on unfinished business) with Gestalt principles, I have identified markers, or process indicators, in Morag's dialogue. First, there are many markers of unfinished business: lingering, unresolved feelings towards significant people in Morag's life that have not been fully owned or expressed. Second, there are markers of conflict splits, whereby family and other influences override Morag's own preferences or needs. She experiences a struggle between the two sides, emotional discomfort and uncertainty. Third, there are markers for self-interruptive splits, or, in FEP terms, over-control of emotion. These indicate schemas, such as: 'I'm not supposed to feel this'; 'I'm supposed to accept life isn't fair'; or 'I'm supposed to be unselfish and help others'. In comments such as 'knotted up', 'trapped' and 'I brought it on myself', Morag identifies that part of herself acts to prevent another part from expressing her emotions and needs.

Therapeutic possibilities

Indications for success in FEP depend on the processing style of the client, rather than on presenting problems. The client may not spontaneously focus on their moment-by-moment inner experience; however, if the therapy succeeds, the client quickly responds to therapist interventions by turning inward and exploring bodily, emotional and cognitive experience. Much of the challenge is to adapt interventions to meet the needs of Morag's particular processing style.

I feel optimistic about working with Morag for several reasons. First, she found the process of answering my questions interesting, and recognized that physical cues could focus her attention on important issues to explore. Second, FEP is specifically designed to help clients who over-control emotion. There are many instances in which Morag demonstrates interruptions of emotional expression, when she hesitates, laughs, speculates about another's feelings or 'looks for intelligent explanations'. However, when she was encouraged to attend to and express physical and emotional experience directly, as in my questions about specific people, she readily did so in an open, honest and clear way, with ownership and with desire for relief from these feelings. These indices are characteristic of healthy expression. I imagine that it will be a challenge to help Morag stay in touch with her own experience in the present; and I am curious to what extent we would achieve that task.

Third, Morag made commitments to work on several areas (outlined in 'Criteria for successful outcome' below) in which an FEP approach could be helpful. I admire her courage, in that she was willing to deepen exploration, despite predictions that she would feel upset (which she finds difficult) and risk herself (or James) feeling hurt or 'attacked'. I hear her honouring and respecting herself (and James) by being willing to take these risks.

Fourth, Morag's awareness of how she handles her emotions, and her spontaneous links between past influences and current values (such as between her mother's 'ethic' and her own attempts to help others), bode well for her capacity to understand her bodily experience in terms of emotional meaning and cognitive schemas. For example, Morag noted the 'important change-over point' in her relationship with Carl. Fifth, Morag is willing to take responsibility for, or to examine, her own contributions to problems; for example, when she says 'I guess I'm my own worst enemy'. Another index that Morag could respond to FEP is that she values her relationship with James as one in which she can have an argument (in contrast to her other partners who did not express feelings).

However, these speculations are guesswork and I am more comfortable with the idea of outlining an experiment and inviting Morag to try it. A refusal would not be a contraindication of success, but an opportunity to learn about predictions, goals or schemas.

I am not conscious of clear contraindications when I imagine working with Morag. I want to convey that she can be herself in therapy (rather than achieving for my sake); that she is responsible only for herself and that she is in control; that it is her time and space. I am curious to know if she will experience relief and/or some fear about that opportunity. I am also interested to see what it will be like for her not to achieve or 'sort out' things or intellectualize (as she does habitually), but simply to experience and express feeling. My sense is that she may benefit from learning about that process, before leaping into action or decisions, because her thoughts and feelings are often disconnected (not concurrently experienced). For example, Morag recounts the lack of appreciation from her father without obvious signs of feeling, and elsewhere mentions feeling hurt by criticism. I am curious to see her reaction if I suggest an experiment in which she imagines her father (as he was in her youth, rather than as he is now) sitting in front of her, so that she might tell him how she feels towards him for never openly expressing feelings or pride in her.

At times, Morag asks questions and may be seeking expert advice. One danger is that she may experience my guidance, to stay with feelings and make sense of them, as a rejection or withholding of help. If Morag seeks advice on content rather than guidance on process, she may have an adverse reaction to internal exploration or to focusing on herself rather than others. It is my guess that this would not be the case.

Morag's motivation to work is set in the context of lifelong scripts, adopted to protect herself and others from acknowledgement and expression of her feelings. She has a right to choose whether or not to work in this model of therapy, and I do not presume the right to judge her decision.

The course of therapy

I might offer Morag a contract of ten meetings of one hour's duration each, with one- and three-month follow-up sessions. We would begin by exploring priorities for work, and while doing so I would ask her to be guided by her bodily reactions. I would invite her to attend to what she does with these feelings in the here-and-now (such as laughing anger off or pushing tears away) and the effects that this has.

We would link these strategies with her experiences as a child by exploring, through guided fantasy, her memories of growing up. We would continue to discover and acknowledge scripts that she adopted to fit her world, such as 'to earn attention I must achieve', or 'if I'm hurt I should attack back, or keep busy'. I would invite Morag to choose whether to maintain these schemas, to re-evaluate them as an adult with the understanding and choices she has now, or to let them go.

As we discussed the scripts, I would ask Morag to catch predictions she makes about expressing feelings, such as 'James will be hurt or attack me'. In an ongoing way, we would work on making our meetings safe, whereby Morag could express feelings without any fear of being criticized. I would want to empower her to make choices for herself, rather than to feel helpless or resentful as she meets the needs of others or earns their approval. I would aim for the therapy to create an opportunity where she gave a voice to the inner feelings that have been suppressed.

We might also talk about pacing, to meet her concern that accessing feelings may be painful. I find it helpful to concentrate on one piece of unfinished business in each session for progress and completion; and Morag would be able to stop at any time. This is particularly important given her drive for achievement, which may pressure her into being a 'good client' and working to the extent that she feels overwhelmed. I might ask Morag to practise ways of recognizing and celebrating her achievements between meetings.

By the third meeting, we would be discussing how to create experiments that might give her some relief. In terms of the unfinished business, I would ask her to choose one relationship to concentrate on in each meeting. The experiment could involve inviting that person in her imagination to sit in a chair facing her, so that she had an opportunity to tell them directly how she feels, without editing emotions. As she did so, I would help her to maintain contact with the significant other and her emotions by offering prompts, such as: 'If it fits, try saying Carl, I feel hurt that you . . .', and I would encourage her to make a list of what hurts. Or I might say: 'Tell Paula what that knot in your throat is saying . . . It's okay to be angry here'. We would continue until Morag felt satisfied that she had done enough – an important aspect to practise in itself. We would discuss what changes, if any, she had experienced, whether in her body, or in terms of scripts or cognitively – for example, that she could express anger without feeling hurt or that she was not to blame. I would aim to explore with her the possibility that she can express feelings in a way that gains relief, without having to depend on someone else to change; and that in doing so, she can feel more self-acceptance and peace.

To summarize the process within each session, we would be likely to move through five steps:

- finding a focus;
- making a commitment to work;
- working (often by 're-entering' a relationship through symbolic empty-chair dialogues to own, express and complete previously interrupted feelings);
- evaluating her work; and
- planning homework (or ways to consolidate her achievements).

In terms of Morag's internal conflicts, we might create a dialogue between the two sides of her, as if they were separate people, in order to slow down her rapid, unconscious process of switching from one side to another over issues about which she feels ambivalent; for example, in feeling resentful of James's expectations, and guilty that she does not do more. As we worked on the dialogue, we would have the opportunity to recognize the needs, wants or values underlying each side of the conflict. With a better understanding of these, and through negotiation between the two sides, we could aim for a more integrated whole.

Problem areas

As an experiential psychotherapy, FEP focuses on the client's ongoing process and their moment-by-moment experiencing, whether of the present or their re-experiencing of the past. This experiencing, and the development of its emotional meaning, are crucial on the path to therapeutic change.

The problems that are paramount are not so much to do with Morag as with the project. While an invaluable exercise, the project assumes that process therapies can use the same data (verbal transcripts) as other approaches. However, transcripts offer content, not process, and FEP is a process model, relying on *how* the client tells her story. Despite intermittent comments on Morag's non-verbal communication by the assessor, I am missing continuous information about her body language, her tone of voice, and indices of developing affect – all essential cues that I rely on for my next question or statement.

To participate in the project, I am forced to make interpretations (on the basis of limited data) and to read between the lines in a way I would not do under normal therapy conditions. While I have tried to remain descriptive, I miss Morag's immediate feedback (non-verbally and verbally). For example, in the first session I would ask directly about her laughter when in contact with feelings and about her difficulty in expressing sadness. Typically, I work on safety with clients, who make individual predictions about their fears of accessing or expressing emotion. These might include hurting others (as Morag fears for James) or being in danger for self (as Morag fears being attacked). Success in identifying and resolving these predictions, so that therapy becomes 'a safe place to play', is crucial for ongoing process and outcome. For example, clients may choose to set their 'critic' or 'judge' outside; others need help to experience being themselves without fear of others' reactions; still others may need guidance to experiment without becoming overwhelmed (by grief or anger). I do not know whether we could have dealt with these immediately so that they did not become problems. But within these and other limitations of the project, I see several dilemmas I would like to address:

1 At some points, Morag focuses on external factors, such as Paula's selfishness, or James's fears, or the reasons Carl prevented her becoming a partner, rather than on her own inner experience. I might invite her to own her values behind this stance; for example, her sensitivity to others, which she mentions learning from her mother. I would invite her to look at its limitations, such as its impact on the recognition of her own feelings. Morag may or may not choose to experiment in therapy by focusing on her own needs, feelings and perceptions; in either case, it is important to evaluate the consequences for her in the present and for the course of therapy.

2 Morag says that she habitually busies herself and rationalizes in response to hurt or fear. She also reports that in 'blowing back' or 'having a moan' she does not really get angry. As an FEP therapist, I do not offer myself as an expert in philosophy. I offer a particular set of beliefs and theories; for example, that feelings are natural, healthy and adaptive. Morag may choose to adopt or reject any one of my principles. She does not need to 'buy' the FEP stance as a whole: she can explore what fits her as a person and what she would like to experiment with (or not). She is more familiar with 'analysing' and 'doing', and may choose to continue with these strategies.

3 Morag sometimes makes statements about other people needing to change, such as James changing his job or criticizing less, or her stepchildren being less selfish. In FEP, I differentiate the expression of Morag's feeling towards them when they do or do not do specific things, from her requests to them to behave differently. Morag may not agree with me that her sense of control, ownership and power to change may depend as much on the

former as the latter; that is, rather than waiting for them to change (and feeling helpless), she can resolve her own feelings and, in doing so, change herself in relation to them. After this expressive work, Morag may feel clearer about what she would like to request of them.

4 I have talked about an individual contract with Morag. However, we might consider joint work with James. In FEP, for example, it may be helpful to explore their communication, with an exercise in which they take turns making statements like: 'I appreciate you for . . .', 'I resent you for . . .', and 'I do not need you to change'. This may be one way to address Morag's dilemma that either she or the other ought to change. Instead, Morag might explore her contribution, for example, to the process of being hurt by criticism (such as its emotional meaning, or that it triggers unfinished business), rather than just asking James to stop criticizing.

Criteria for successful outcome

I am asked to comment on my criteria for success in this case. In FEP, the client is viewed as the expert on her own experience and the only person in a position to evaluate therapy. She is asked at the outset what she would like to achieve (to my shame, I forgot to relay this question!) and, when specific points of focus arise, the client is asked whether or not she would make a commitment to work on this theme.

In the first interview, Morag begins by describing two main areas in which she would like help. First, she describes feeling aggressive towards her stepchildren, and wants to be able to 'be cool and think it doesn't matter'. She is also unsure whether she should be 'getting them to understand' what she feels. Second, Morag wants to focus on her level of activity, which she enjoys but recognizes that it causes conflict with James. She asks, 'Is it right that I should always be wanting . . . some new challenge? Should I just be accepting the way I am?'. And later, 'Should I try not to do quite so much . . . for the happiness of the relationship?' In extending this theme, Morag says she would like to improve the situation. She expresses uncertainty about the degree to which she is responsible for James's unhappiness, but goes on: 'The problem is one would like to be able to change oneself to suit someone else – but at the end of the day you cannot do that'.

As the interview proceeds, Morag defines two further areas in which she may want help. Talking about her feelings towards Paula, Morag refers to 'something that I have been totally – not exactly puzzled by, because I think it's almost a biological thing'. She describes 'knotting up' and 'feeling cross' when Paula's name is mentioned. However, Morag also says: 'I suppose I feel that my anger to her, if you like, I can contain. Not contain, but it doesn't affect my life that often'. I am unclear at this stage whether her feelings towards Paula need to be a focus for therapy or not.

Finally, Morag says quietly, and with affect and silences: 'Maybe I should do a bit of exorcism on the Carl time', so that she could 'go on and do something else'. And she continues: 'But how do you do that? I'm not quite sure'.

Morag's goals are extracted as much as possible at a descriptive level. I want to clarify each goal through questions such as: 'So you want to work on . . .' and 'What would you like to achieve?' Her answers would help guide my therapeutic strategies, such as in the experiments I offer her. Through my questions, the assessor tried the beginning of a series of experiments on my behalf, and asked Morag if she would like to continue to focus on specific relationships.

She made a clear commitment to work on her feelings towards James ('Yes, sure') and she aimed for 'a greater understanding', 'different reactions' and 'more peace and harmony'. She also clearly wanted to work on feelings towards Carl, and felt 'hopeful', although 'unsure what the outcome would be'. She wanted to sort out her feelings towards her stepchildren, and felt 'optimistic' that she could feel 'less aggressive'. Her response – 'mm' – to an invitation to address her feelings towards Paula is unclear. I would have followed it up with 'Is that yes or no?'. However – and I am guessing here – her readiness to talk indicated some commitment.

One way in which Morag and I might evaluate success would be to review these goals. However, FEP rests on evaluation as an integral part of the work, so I would continually invite Morag to attend to her present experience in the session – physical, emotional and cognitive changes that can indicate that we are off-beam or on the right track for her. Similarly, at the end of each session, I would invite Morag to evaluate her work by asking her to attend to physical changes, new perceptions and shifts in emotional meaning, within and outside a particular relationship upon which we have focused.

Summary

The following diagram briefly illustrates the process Morag might move through in an experiment on unfinished business:

Morag experiences lingering, unresolved feelings
↓
expresses blame, regret or bitterness
↓
differentiates feelings of anger and sadness
(accessing different memories in the present)
↓
expressions of specific emotions intensify
↓
owns and expresses unmet needs
↓
resolution, self-affirmation, new view of others

Morag summarizes the work and aims of FEP better than I could in her statement that she needs to 'do a bit of exorcism (of the feelings) on the Carl time' so that she can 'go on and do something else'. In FEP, I believe that by clearing our unfinished business, we accept ourselves and release the energy used to suppress feelings, so that it can be reinvested in new relationships and new ways of being.

Further reading

Daldrup, R.J. and Gust, D. (1988). *Freedom from Anger.* New York: Pocket Books.

Daldrup, R.J., Beutler, L.E., Engle, D. and Greenberg, L.S. (1988). *Focused Expressive Psychotherapy: Freeing the Over Controlled Patient.* New York: Guilford Press.

Greenberg, L.S., Rise, L.N. and Elliott, R. (1993). *Facilitating Emotional Change: The Moment-by-moment Process.* New York: Guilford Press.

Hobson, R.F. (1985). *Forms of Feeling: The Heart of Psychotherapy.* London: Tavistock.

Mahoney, M.J. (1991). *Human Change Processes: The Scientific Foundations of Psychotherapy.* New York: Basic Books.

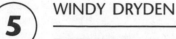

WINDY DRYDEN

RATIONAL EMOTIVE BEHAVIOUR THERAPY

Introduction

Before I begin to describe my work with Morag, let me briefly mention my reservations about contributing to this volume. First, I find it difficult to convey my work with a client in case-study format, even when I know that client intimately, without illustrating the write-up with verbatim transcript material. As the reader knows, none of the therapists have met Morag and our communications with her have been through Moira Walker. If I find case studies difficult to write when I know my client, imagine my difficulty when I have not even communicated directly with Morag.

Second, the part of the process where I raised questions with Morag through Moira Walker had its attendant frustrations for me. Morag did not grasp the meaning of several of my questions and where, in direct communication, I would have had the opportunity to explain what I meant or phrase the questions in a different way, this avenue was closed to me here. Also, several of Morag's answers were not clear to me and I had no opportunity for seeking clarification. Thus, the struggle for understanding, which is such an essential part of the counselling process, is entirely absent here.

Finally, I have a specific concern relating to Morag's personal circumstances. Her husband has had the experience of losing his first wife, as he saw it, as a consequence of counselling. According to Morag, he gets angry and agitated at the very mention of the word 'counselling'. In the light of this, and in answer to one of my questions, Morag is reluctant to involve her husband in couple counselling and does not want to tell him of her involvement in this project. This is, of course, her right and I respect this right. While it is unlikely that her husband will learn of this project, it is not impossible that he will find out about it and I shudder to think of the aftermath of such a discovery. Fay Weldon's (1994) novel *Affliction* raises a host of questions about the impact of individual therapy on the health of a marriage and, while, of course, Morag's involvement in this project does not constitute therapy, it is in the public domain and I raise this concern because I am troubled by it.

I wish to stress that by raising these concerns at the outset, I am not looking for excuses to explain away any failure on my part to discern Morag's therapeutic needs and my ability to meet them. Rather, I wish to voice my concerns so that the reader can understand my doubts. Having disclosed them, I can turn my full attention to the task.

The therapist

My formal training in counselling began in 1974 when I started the one-year full-time Diploma in Counselling in Educational Settings course at Aston University. While this course was basically person-centred, we studied a range of therapeutic approaches and, in particular, we had an excellent grounding in behavioural counselling. While this course taught me the importance of the core conditions, I also discovered from my placement experiences that many clients wanted more specific help than person-centred counselling seemed to offer them. I thought that psychodynamic therapy would provide this missing ingredient, so I enrolled on a two-year part-time course on psychodynamic therapy at the Uffculme Clinic in Birmingham. I soon discovered that I was neither temperamentally suited to this approach, nor did I resonate intellectually with its major ideas. So, in 1977, I changed tack and pursued training in what was known then as rational-emotive therapy (see Dryden 1991, for a fuller discussion of my reasons for doing so).

While I have practised what is now known as rational emotive behaviour therapy (REBT) ever since, in that I use its rich theory to guide my interventions, my approach to counselling and psychotherapy is informed by other therapeutic developments which I believe enrich my practice and make me a more flexible practitioner than I would be if I was only informed by REBT theory. Let me give thumbnail sketches of these influences so that the reader can get a sense of my therapeutic practice. I begin by outlining REBT.

Rational emotive behaviour therapy

Rational emotive behaviour therapy is an active-directive approach to psychotherapy, which states that at the core of psychological problems is the following set of irrational beliefs:

1 *Dogmatic musts and shoulds*: the task of the therapist here is to help clients dispute these rigid beliefs and stay with their healthy flexible preferences.
2 *Awfulizing*: here, the therapist's task is to help clients to evaluate negative events as 'bad', but not 'awful'.
3 *Low frustration tolerance*: here, the therapist encourages her clients to raise their level of frustration tolerance and to see that they can put up with frustration when it is in their interests to do so.
4 *Damning self and others*: here, the therapist encourages her clients to accept themselves and others as fallible human beings who cannot legitimately be given a global rating.

In carrying out these tasks, the REBT therapist draws on a large variety of cognitive, emotive and behavioural techniques and uses them flexibly, while helping her clients achieve their healthy therapeutic goals.

Therapeutic alliance theory

Ed Bordin (1979) published a seminal paper on the alliance between client and therapist in which he distinguished between three main domains of the alliance. The first domain represents the bond which develops between client and therapist. There are several dimensions of the therapeutic bond that are salient here, including the degree to which the client perceives the therapist as showing high levels of the core conditions, the relevance of the therapist's influence base (likeability or expertise) and the success or otherwise of the match between the therapist's and the client's interpersonal style. Here, successful therapy tends to occur when the bond formed between client and therapist promotes effective goal-directed therapeutic work. The second domain concerns the goals of therapy. Here effective therapy tends to occur when therapist and client agree on the client's goals and these goals are in the client's healthy interests. Finally, the third domain relates to the tasks of therapy. According to therapeutic alliance theory, both therapist and client have tasks to perform during therapy. Successful therapy tends to occur when the client understands his own and the therapist's tasks, when the therapeutic tasks are relevant and potent, when the client can execute his tasks effectively and when the therapist carries out his tasks skilfully.

Technical eclecticism

I have also been influenced by Arnold Lazarus's (1989) views on technical eclecticism. Working from the perspective of social learning theory, Lazarus puts forward four significant ideas. First, he argues that it is important to use techniques that have been tested and shown to be effective in research trials. Second, although for a number of client problems a variety of therapeutic approaches will prove beneficial, in other cases specific problems require specific interventions. Third, when using techniques that originate from specific schools of psychotherapy, it is not necessary to adopt the theoretical perspective of the approach that spawned the technique in question. In this respect, I regard REBT as a form of theoretically consistent eclecticism, in that when I use two-chair dialogue (a gestalt therapy technique), for example, I do so for a therapeutic purpose that is consistent with REBT theory (rather than with gestalt theory, in this case). Finally, it is important to consider a broad range of modalities when working therapeutically with clients. Lazarus mentions behaviour, affect, sensation, imagery, cognition, interpersonal relations and biology as the seven major modalities that may need therapeutic attention.

Further information requested

At the outset of psychotherapy, I begin by asking a client to describe why she is seeking help at this time. As the client talks, I clarify my understanding of what she is saying and begin to ask questions to gain a detailed understanding of what is going on in her life. During this period, I make a decision concerning whether and which questionnaires to ask her to complete, the purpose of which is to deepen my understanding of her problems and what might account for them. In the absence of an opportunity to carry out a face-to-face interview with Morag, I decided to ask her to complete a detailed Life History Inventory (Lazarus and Lazarus 1991), two belief questionnaires, a stage of change questionnaire to determine which stage of change she was in, and a questionnaire to determine how she construed her problems and what might be most helpful to her in counselling. I want to stress that I do not normally ask clients to complete such a range of questionnaires. I am aware now of wanting to compensate for the lack of information I had to hand about Morag and for the lack of opportunity of interviewing her directly. This demonstrates a tendency that I have of being somewhat obsessive as a clinician when faced with this level of ambiguity and uncertainty.

Having received the completed questionnaires and taking Morag's answers together with the transcript of the first interview, I asked for the following additional information. Again I am aware of going over the top here, thus revealing again my obsessive tendency as a therapist under ambiguous conditions.

Relationship with James (her partner)
Here I wanted to know how valuable it would be if James were to be involved in therapy with Morag. Her reply, in fact, evaded the question, saying that he would not wish to be so involved rather than commenting on the value of any involvement. It was here that she said about James:

> He blames counsellors for the split-up of his first marriage, or
> his marriage, and although I say it wouldn't have happened
> like that, and that his wife is manipulative – you know –
> when she said that the counsellor told her to leave him she,
> the counsellor, wouldn't have done that, unless they were a
> very bad one, um . . . he feels, you've only just got to
> mention counsellors or counselling and he gets really angry,
> so he wouldn't come.

In reply to some questions about their tolerance of the differences between them, Morag again did not quite capture the meaning of my question and commented that they both try to accommodate to one another, and that probably 'neither of us realize how much effort the other person does put in'. Here I was interested in their attitude rather than their efforts.

Feelings about Paula (James's ex-wife)
In the first interview, Morag says that she feels 'myself inside sort of knotting up' when she hears Paula's name mentioned. I asked for more precise information about this feeling, to which Morag replies 'angry but wary' (which I do not quite understand) and then goes on to say that she is angry about Paula's hopelessness (which she sees as a selfish device), her manipulativeness and her 'mother's lack of overwhelming concern for children'. What might lie behind such anger can only be discerned by careful interviewing.

Feelings of guilt
REBT therapists keenly distinguish between guilt (which involves self-blame) and healthy remorse (where a person takes responsibility for her wrongdoing, does not blame her 'self', but feels remorseful about what she did). I tried to phrase this so Morag could tell me whether her experience of guilt is guilt or healthy remorse by my definition. Unfortunately, she did not understand this distinction and thus I can only speculate on which emotion she experiences

when she speaks of guilt. In reply to a question asking for a list of what she feels guilty about, Morag says:

> Guilty that I don't spend enough time on James. Guilty that I don't spend enough time on my daughter. Guilty that I don't spend enough time on my mother. Guilty that I don't spend enough time on my work, that I don't spend enough time on the catering business. Guilty that I don't spend enough time on the house. Guilty that I don't spend enough time on myself [*laughs*]. Um . . . I think that about covers it [*laughs again*].

Seeking new challenges

In the first interview, Morag asks: 'Is it right that I should always be wanting something new to go at, some new challenge?' In answer to my enquiry why she thinks that it might not be right for her to seek new challenges, Morag replies that new challenges involve commitment on her time; thus, if she makes such a commitment, she experiences a 'backlog' of things that she has to cope with and do.

Selfishness

The word 'selfish' often cropped up in Morag's replies to the questionnaires that I sent her and elsewhere. I asked her to elaborate on the meaning of this concept for her. She sees Paula and her father as having a similar form of selfishness, in that they think about themselves primarily and everybody else comes definitely a long way down the list. She sees her stepchildren's selfishness as 'the selfishness of youth, in that they can't see the sort of perhaps longer-term implications of their actions'. She says that she sees her own selfishness in terms of guilt and relates it to being a fairly directed person who can decide where she is going and doing it. Presumably, the guilt she experiences as a result of going for what she wants is explained in her response to my earlier question concerning what she feels guilty about in her life.

In response to my query concerning what she finds so upsetting about the selfishness of others, Morag said: 'The selfishness of others: it puts burdens on other people, really, that come into the sphere of activity. Selfishness of myself: I suppose that's the same thing. It makes people unhappy if I'm selfish'.

Criticism

Morag mentions having difficulties dealing with criticism in the first interview, and twice on the Life History Inventory. Thus she completes the sentence 'one of the ways people hurt me is . . .' by saying 'being critical'; and she says in response to the question 'When are you most likely to lose control of your feelings?', 'When criticized and when faced with aggressive behaviour'. So I asked her, 'What is it about being criticized that is upsetting to you?' Morag said in response: 'That I'm not doing as well as I should be'. She also mentioned that she would like help in dealing with and handling criticism more effectively.

Stress at work
Morag mentioned in the first interview that she experiences stress at work. She was not explicit about this, so I asked her what she finds stressful at work. Her reply was long and somewhat difficult to follow, but what I got from it was this. First, when she employed other people she considered herself responsible for them at a time when she did not have enough work and wished she could do something to help them. Second, she finds it stressful when her staff do not work to her own standards. As a result, she has to pick up the pieces that follow, which includes explaining the situation to her clients. On the one hand she knows that people can only work to their own ability, but on the other my hunch is that she is intolerant when they do not work to her standards. She also realizes that she has made life difficult at home by bringing her stress home with her. She reports having made some changes to cope with work stress by not working with others and by saying 'no' when she gets overloaded.

Pressure
I picked up in several places that Morag puts herself under pressure to do well and drives herself very hard. Knowing that clients are often ambivalent about changing such patterns, I asked the following question: 'What advantages and disadvantages do you see if you put yourself under less pressure to do well or stop driving yourself so hard?' Morag says in reply:

> Um . . . I'd be er, probably be less aggressive. I'd be more gentle. I mean if I go back to the time when I stopped working and I had Jessica, um . . . I mean, the atmosphere was definitely . . . you know, if you've got more time, and you're not rushing from one thing to another thing, you don't have such a short fuse. Yes I know I'm my own worst enemy in . . . in . . . you know, because for example, I've not only got the accountancy business, I've also got the catering business, and I took that on willingly [*laughs*] and I enjoy a

challenge. I suppose that's a problem, that if I don't have anything else, if I just had, you know ... er ... er ... domestic sort of stuff, I think I'd cope with it for a while, but er ... I think that sooner or later that I'd get pretty fed up with it.

I will discuss other relevant information, particularly from the questionnaires I sent Morag, in other sections of this chapter.

Assessment

I wish to stress at the outset that any assessment hypotheses that I put forward in this section are just that – they are hypotheses. I will put them to Morag and emphasize that we will work together as a team in sharpening up our joint formulation of her concerns. With this in mind, let me share my understanding of what Morag is grappling with based on the initial interview and the material I requested from her.

Challenge-seeking versus discharging responsibilities

The form of words that the editor chose to represent Morag's dilemma ('myself or mother-hen') will probably be a central feature of her therapy, although I might phrase it a little differently. Morag seems to be struggling to reconcile her strong desire for seeking challenges on the one hand, with her responsibilities towards others on the other. Temperamentally, Morag seems to be a very active individual. At work she seems at her happiest when faced with a challenge and, when bored, she seeks out new challenges. Once she has decided to do something, she goes for it. At this point, however, another dynamic comes into play and this concerns Morag's standards. She expects from herself and from others with whom she is associated, particularly at work, a high standard of performance. Although she understands intellectually that others (e.g. the people whom she employs) can only work to the level of their ability, my hunch is that she is somewhat intolerant when they do not take into account factors that might bring them up to scratch. It seems to me that Morag abhors hopelessness in people, when they do not acknowledge and adjust to their limitations. This helps to explain her strong antipathy towards Paula (James's ex-wife).

On the other hand, it seems to me that Morag has a keen sense of her responsibilities towards others, particularly with respect to the time she spends on them. One just has to look at the list of people and things that she feels guilty about with respect to her failure to spend time on them, to get a sense of what she is struggling with here. Morag needs to clone herself if she is to solve her dilemma without recourse to inner change.

What happens to Morag concerning this dilemma is probably something like this. The more she actualizes her challenge-seeking side, the more she becomes aware of not fulfilling her responsibilities to her family, for example. However, the more time she spends on these responsibilities, the more she experiences a sense of being unfulfilled, which activates her yearning for challenge.

The question that I ask myself at this point concerns whether or not Morag has emotional problems about one or both sides of her conflict. I will determine this by discovering how Morag feels when she fails to actualize her active, challenge-seeking self on the one hand, and when she fails to actualize her responsible self on the other. REBT theory distinguishes between healthy and unhealthy negative emotions. Thus, when Morag thinks about or actually fails to actualize her challenge-seeking self, it is healthy for her to experience disappointment, annoyance, concern, sadness and remorse. These negative emotions are healthy in the sense that they indicate that her healthy desires are not being met and that they motivate her to reflect on the situation that she is in and change what can be changed. However, if Morag were to experience hurt, anger, anxiety, depression and guilt when thinking about or actually failing to seek challenges, then these would be regarded as unhealthy negative emotions in REBT, in that they indicate that her unhealthy demands are not being met. They tend to get in the way of her reflecting constructively on what needs to be changed.

As an REBT therapist, I need to know whether Morag experiences unhealthy or healthy negative feelings when she is not able to actualize the challenge-seeking side of herself. I need to know this to determine whether or not she has irrational beliefs about the frustration of her challenge-seeking side. Unfortunately, from the information available to me, I do not know precisely the nature of Morag's emotions when the challenge-seeking part of herself is frustrated. Thus, I cannot make an accurate assessment statement on this issue.

I also need to know how Morag feels when she fails to discharge her responsibilities with respect to the time she spends on significant people and important things in her life. Morag says that she feels guilty about her failures in this area. However, as an REBT therapist, I know that when a person says that she feels guilty, she may mean one of three things: first, she may mean that she blames herself for her wrongdoing; second, she may mean that she is remorseful, but not self-blaming about it; and third, she may also use 'feeling guilty' to mean being guilty of a wrongdoing without referring to any emotion. My attempt to distinguish between unhealthy guilt and healthy remorse for Morag in my follow-up list of questions was met with incomprehension on her part. This means that I cannot make an accurate assessment statement on this point either.

The point to bear in mind is that it is only possible for me to make an accurate assessment of the presence or absence of Morag's unhealthy and healthy negative emotions on the one hand, and of her rational and irrational beliefs on the other, by careful interviewing where I explain in detail the distinctions between the two types of negative emotions and the two types of beliefs. Once Morag understands these distinctions, she can use them as a yardstick against which she can judge her experiences in concrete situations. This point is important. As an REBT therapist, I can only really make an accurate assessment of Morag's concerns by looking at concrete examples of these concerns that are rooted in time and space.

This point is particularly apposite for someone like Morag who, I think, presents herself as more together than she really is. Note, for example, how controlled she is at the start of the first interview. Also, on one of the belief questionnaires that I asked her to complete, which is particularly designed to gauge a person's rational and irrational beliefs, Morag's responses indicated a low incidence of irrational beliefs. However, these items are phrased in general terms and therefore may not tap instances of specific irrational beliefs that Morag may hold in specific situations. Again this information can only be determined accurately by careful interviewing.

Finally, Morag may have an emotional problem about the dilemma itself. Thus, she may believe that she absolutely should not be in conflict or that other people must change to accommodate her. Or she may have a set of rational beliefs about her conflict. Once again, only face-to-face interviewing will reveal the answer to this question.

Standards and accomplishments

There is some evidence that Morag adds to her own stress by her attitude towards achievement and the standards of performance that she sets for herself. By taking on so much, Morag believes with some justification that she must perform well, otherwise things get out of hand. However, from some of her replies to the questionnaires that I sent her and from the Life History Inventory, there is some evidence that she adds to this stress by having difficulty settling for second best. Thus she signalled agreement with the following items on the Life History Inventory:

- 'I should be good at everything I do'.
- 'I should strive for perfection'.

However, on the belief questionnaires she indicated a mixture of agreement and disagreement with items referring to demands for achievement, accomplishment and perfection. I will need to take this up with her in the early phase of therapy and clarify her position on striving to accomplish and to do well.

Selfishness

The concept of selfishness is referred to a lot in the material that I was sent, and by Morag. My hypothesis is that a large part of her anger towards her stepchildren and James's ex-wife concerns her demand that they must not be selfish. I will need to confirm or disconfirm this during therapy, but there is sufficient evidence to support this hypothesis in the material for me to be more confident on this point than I am on some of the other hunches that I have so far put forward. At various points, Morag describes the following people as selfish: her stepchildren, Paula, her father and herself. However, she particularly feels angry towards the selfishness displayed by Paula and her stepchildren, mainly because 'such selfishness places additional burdens on others' and 'makes them unhappy'. Whether this is the full story is difficult to say. In therapy, I will use an assessment procedure called 'inference chaining' designed to help us both identify the precise aspect of other people's selfishness about which Morag is most angry.

Autonomy and space versus affiliation and approval

Another reason why Morag feels aggressive when her stepchildren come at the weekend is because she feels 'very crowded'. She also mentions on one of the belief questionnaires that the following have been mostly true for a major part of her life: 'I do feel I can cope well by myself' and 'I hate to be constrained or kept from doing what I want'. On the other hand, she also longs for affiliation and approval. Thus, she says of her relationship with James: 'I'm fairly determined that I want this relationship to stay, and you know, to grow old together'; the editor records that 'her eyes water and she goes quiet'. Interestingly, the only other time in the first interview that Morag showed emotion was when she spoke about Carl, her previous partner. Also, she endorses the following item as being mostly true of her for a major part of her life: 'I worry about pleasing other people'.

How does this dilemma come into play for Morag? At some point, being with others activates her need for space and autonomy, whereas pursuing her autonomous activities leads others to raise objections which activate her worry about them being displeased with her. When asked on the Life History Inventory to name any two wishes, one of these shows how Morag would ideally like to solve this dilemma: 'I would like to buy a rambling old house with a huge garden beside an estuary, with plenty of room for everyone to be on their own'. Given Morag's interest in 'doing up' houses, notice also what a challenge it would be to do up such a house!

As with her dilemma of challenge-seeking versus discharging her responsibilities, I need to determine to what extent Morag has emotional problems about each part of the conflict as well as the dilemma itself. With the information that I have available to me, I cannot make an authoritative statement on this point.

Other issues

It is clear that Morag has other concerns. However, I will mention two which may well feature prominently in therapy.

1 *Unfinished business with Carl, her previous partner.* One of the reasons why she still feels so sad about that relationship is that before she learned of Carl's affair, this relationship provided her with both loving affiliation and challenge, a combination which is not present in her relationship with James.
2 *Her relationship with James.* It is with James that a number of the issues I have discussed come into play. For example, it is interesting that he was first drawn to her by her independence, but that now he wants her to look after him. This change in the 'rules of the relationship' activates Morag's dilemmas in ways that I have already described.

Therapeutic possibilities

In this section, I consider the therapeutic possibilities in Morag's case. To help me in this I asked Morag to complete the Stages of Change questionnaire and the Opinion about Psychological Problems questionnaire.

Stages of Change questionnaire

Morag's responses on the Stages of Change questionnaire indicated that she considers that she does have problems, that she has already taken some steps to overcome them and, indeed, is working to maintain the gains where these steps have proven successful. Since it is not clear what steps Morag has taken to help herself, nor do I know what effect her self-change efforts have had, I will assess these points at the outset of therapy. I will do this so that I can capitalize on those efforts at self-help that are productive for Morag in the short and long term and explain why other self-change methods may be less productive for her.

There are some puzzling responses on this questionnaire which require clarification. Thus, Morag states that she agrees with the items 'I think I might be ready for some self-improvement' and 'I am doing something about the problems that have been bothering me', but disagrees with the items 'I've been thinking that I might want to change something about myself' and 'I am finally doing some work on my problems'. I do not understand this apparent contradiction in response and I will clarify this with Morag at the beginning of therapy.

Despite the above puzzle, it is clear to me that Morag is a good candidate for psychotherapy, but is she a good candidate for REBT?

Suitability for REBT

To attempt to answer this question, I asked Morag to complete the Opinion about Psychological Problems (OPP) questionnaire, which assesses potential clients' views on the causes of their psychological problems and what might help them overcome these problems. The items are grouped according to the following different ways of understanding and dealing with such problems: psychodynamic, humanistic, behavioural, cognitive, organic, social/economic and naïve.

Morag's responses show the following. She demonstrates a slight preference for psychodynamic and humanistic explanations of her psychological problems, and while she resonates with all four therapeutic approaches to psychological help, she shows a relatively strong preference for active behavioural interventions. This latter finding is not surprising given Morag's no-nonsense, goal-directed approach to her own life.

While Morag seemingly does not favour a cognitive conceptualization of her psychological problems, which might pose problems for me as an REBT therapist, this may be an artifact of the wording of some of the cognitive items on the OPP. Thus, Morag disagrees with the view that her psychological problems are caused by illogical beliefs and unrealistic thinking (although she does agree that learning to think realistically would be helpful to her). This does not surprise me, since I would expect Morag to balk at the terms 'illogical' and 'unrealistic' when applied to her beliefs. This does mean that she does not hold such beliefs; rather, she objects to the words used to describe them. I will need to explore this with her when I explain the REBT approach that I take as a therapist.

Finally, the responses Morag gives regarding her expectations of therapy on the Life History Inventory are compatible with REBT as a therapy and hopefully with me as an REBT therapist. Here she says that therapy is about helping a client 'arrive at an understanding of why they feel the way they do' and should last 'until a clear understanding of problems is reached so that a way forward can be planned'. Finally, Morag believes that the ideal therapist should be 'caring, able to see through to the root of a problem, analytical, perceptive and a good communicator'.

Individual or couple therapy

While I will initially see Morag for individual therapy, there is probably good reason to hold some conjoint therapy sessions with her partner. As I discussed earlier in this chapter, Morag's dilemmas and problems do get played out in the context of her relationship with James and thus it is sensible to do some therapeutic work in that context if possible. However, I doubt whether conjoint sessions will occur (either with me or another REBT therapist), given Morag's account of James's attitude towards counsellors. Nevertheless, if Morag and I considered it crucial, with her permission I might write to James to invite him to attend for one session at least. James blames his ex-wife's counsellor for the break up of his marriage, but this may be because he was not involved in the therapeutic process. He may thus welcome the opportunity to participate in therapy rather than be an anxious outsider. I say all this knowing that Morag will probably not choose to tell James about being in therapy. If this is the case, I will, of course, respect her decision.

The course of therapy

When I meet with Morag for the first time, I will suggest that we set an agenda for the session and for our subsequent meetings. This is to ensure that therapy is a collaborative endeavour. I will indicate that I wish to hear about why she is seeking help at this time and what she wishes to achieve from seeing me. As we discuss her concerns, I will begin to construct a problem list and suggest that we both keep a copy of this so that we both know what she wishes to address in therapy. I will point out that this list may well be updated as we deal with certain issues and as others may arise. I would imagine that Morag's initial problem list will look something like this.

1 Aggression towards stepchildren.
2 Upset at the mention of Paula's name.
3 James wanting me to spend more time on the family.
4 Boredom with domestic chores and needing a challenge.

This list represents Morag's concerns as she sees them. Each problem will need to be assessed according to the ABC's of REBT (where A stands for an actual or inferred *activating* event, B represents Morag's *belief* about this event and C is the emotional and/or behavioural *consequence* of B).

At the beginning of therapy, I will explain about REBT and what it has to offer, perhaps taking one of Morag's concerns to illustrate this approach in action. I will also invite Morag to raise any concerns about therapy and answer any questions she may have about the process. I will discuss the concept of confidentiality and its exceptions and offer an initial contract of between five and ten sessions, so that she may judge whether REBT is an approach to her concerns that she could profitably use. If it is, we will renegotiate the contract at that point. As is my custom, however, I will probably explain that there are different approaches to therapy. If REBT turns out not to be helpful, or if she considers that she cannot work with me, I will be happy to effect a suitable referral.

When Morag tells me of her concerns, I will strive to demonstrate my understanding of them from her frame of reference and endeavour to show her unconditional acceptance. However, fairly soon into the process we will have to determine whether Morag experiences only dissatisfaction about the major events in her life or whether she is disturbed about them. According to REBT theory, if Morag was dissatisfied (but not disturbed) about the mention of Paula's name, for example, she would experience a healthy negative emotion such as annoyance or disappointment. However, if she had an emotional problem about hearing Paula's name, then she would experience an unhealthy negative emotion such as anger or hurt. It is important for us to determine fairly soon whether or not Morag has a set of emotional problems (rather than healthy dissatisfactions) about the major events in her life, since this will very much guide my therapeutic endeavours.

Thus, if Morag is healthily dissatisfied about her life, I will work with her to discover ways in which she can become more satisfied, for example, by re-evaluating her priorities, reducing her workload, rethinking her expectations of herself and other people and negotiating with significant others, such as James, so that they both get more of what they want from each other if this is possible. In Morag's case, much of this work will be done to help her to minimize the self-defeating aspects of her dilemmas. Thus, if dissatisfaction is the sole therapeutic issue, I will help Morag to see that she can look at specific situations from the vantage point of the full picture of her different desires. When another exciting work opportunity comes her way, I will help her to stand back and weigh up the short- and long-term pros and cons of grasping it given her total workload and her other life commitments. From an REBT perspective, therapy of Morag's life dissatisfactions when she is not emotionally disturbed about the negative aspects of situations that give rise to these dissatisfactions will tend to go relatively smoothly. Since it is now free from the disabling impact of emotional problems, Morag will have sufficient objectivity to see her life as a whole and to weigh up the pros and cons of various, seemingly conflicting courses of action.

However, if Morag experiences emotional problems about any of her life dissatisfactions, then therapy becomes more complicated, since she is less likely to be able to focus on her dissatisfactions when she experiences one or more unhealthy negative emotions. If this is the case, and I have already explained my difficulty in determining whether or not Morag has emotional problems as well as life dissatisfactions, then therapy will proceed differently. Assuming that Morag does have one or more emotional problems, I will give her a rationale why these need to be tackled first (along the lines of the argument put forward at the beginning of this paragraph). If she accepts this, then I will use the REBT sequence developed by my colleague Ray DiGiuseppe and myself (Dryden and DiGiuseppe 1990).

First, I will help Morag to choose one of her emotional problems on which we can focus. This is known as a target problem. I will encourage Morag to give me a typical, specific example of the target problem which I will then assess using the ABC framework (described above). Then I will ensure that Morag understands the link between her irrational beliefs and her dysfunctional responses at C, before proceeding to help her to dispute these beliefs. Here, I might well employ socratic questioning more frequently than didactic explanation, since my guess is that Morag will respond better to such questioning than to didactic exposition (1) because she is bright and articulate and can probably engage profitably with the socratic method, and (2) because this method of disputing is less intrusive and is less likely to invoke Morag's 'reactance' (i.e. her tendency to resist influence attempts that she construes as constraining).

While employing socratic disputing methods, I will make use of empirical, logical and pragmatic questions and monitor Morag's responses to see which she is most responsive to. I will then use these questions more frequently than the others. I will work in this way until Morag has so-called 'intellectual insight' into the dys-functionality of her irrational beliefs and the functionality of her alternative rational beliefs, which I will help her to construct as part of the disputing process. I will then help Morag to see that, in order for her to internalize this new set of rational beliefs so that she develops so-called 'emotional insight' in them, she will need to use a plethora of methods to help her in this internalization process. Thus, using therapeutic alliance theory, I will review with her the major cognitive, emotive, imaginal and behavioural techniques that are available to her as potential change-provoking homework as-signments. These will need to be tailored to her special circum-stances and she will need to see their relevance in helping her to achieve her therapeutic goals before I expect she will choose to do them. However, I predict that once Morag sees the sense in doing something, then she can be relied on to do it given her goal-directed active approach to life, assuming that no obstacles exist to assign-ment completion. If such obstacles do exist, then I will endeavour to engage Morag in an open problem-solving discussion of how she can overcome them.

After we have employed several of these sequences, we will both be clearer about what has been achieved and our contract can be re-negotiated at this point. If we decide to continue to work together, then I will increasingly encourage Morag to take the lead in using the REBT emotional problem-solving sequence when discussing her emotional problems in therapy. Here it is my goal to encourage Morag to become her own therapist. After we have made significant progress on helping her to overcome her emotional problems, then I imagine that we will tackle her dissatisfactions along the lines outlined earlier in this section.

As Morag continues to make progress, I will suggest perhaps re-ducing the frequency of sessions to encourage her to develop even greater responsibility for her self-change efforts. Here, my work is akin to that of a consultant helping Morag to generalize her gains to other similar situations, working with her to trouble-shoot pos-sible problems and to institute relapse prevention measures. If our work is successful, then Morag will have achieved most of her goals, or at least be well on the way towards achieving them. What is more, she will have acquired a self-change methodology, which she will hopefully be able to use to deal with future problems. Whether Morag is able to achieve such a salubrious outcome remains to be seen, and no doubt we will encounter problems along the way. What form might some of these problems take?

Problem areas

Once again it is difficult for me to specify what problems I am likely to face in therapy with Morag without having met her. Also, I have been a therapist long enough to know that seemingly easy cases can turn out to be difficult, while other cases, which at first seem difficult, turn out to be fairly straightforward. One of my toughest ever cases was a couple who were holding hands and gazing lovingly into each other's eyes when I came to collect them from the waiting room for their first session. So any predictions that I make about possible problem areas in my work with Morag are liable to be proved wrong! Conversely, I will probably not even mention areas that may well prove to be problematic.

That caveat expressed, the first area that may prove to be problematic is my gender. Would Morag be better served working with a female therapist with whom she can talk woman-to-woman about what it is like trying 'to do and have it all'? While I will attempt to be empathic to her concerns, will she see me as a man who, like her partner, is trying to encourage her to be a 'mother-hen'? This, of course, is not my intention, but since I will be raising the issue of making compromises between on the one hand going for everything that she wants and being overstressed as a result, and on the other giving up on one significant area and consequently being bored and frustrated, my intention here may be misconstrued by her. As a therapist who believes in checking out such matters explicitly, I will raise the issue with Morag, but I may experience such a problem on this issue.

Second, I wonder to what extent Morag will resonate with the cognitive focus of REBT? From her responses to the OPP and from her pre-existing coping style, I predict that she will find its behavioural thrust helpful, but what will she make of the role that irrational beliefs play in her life? Also, the use of such words as 'irrational' are problematic for a number of women, who have been told by men that they are irrational when they become upset; and of course this pejorative use of the term is very different from its meaning in REBT, where it points to attitudes that interfere with a person pursuing her basic goals and purposes. I will bring this point out into the open with Morag, since I believe that it may be a problem area. I am quite comfortable about using her language to capture the self-limiting inflexible nature of such beliefs. However, the terminology of REBT may lead to problems between us.

The biggest problem that I anticipate in my work with Morag, though, arises out of the non-participation of her partner in therapy. In my experience, whenever a client's partner is involved in that person's problems, there is reason to involve the partner in counselling at some point in the process. The value of doing so differs from case to case. In some situations, educating the partner about the nature of the client's problems is helpful, whereas in others, the greatest benefit comes from discussing and resolving conflicting expectations. I believe that Morag and James come into the latter category. There may be a limit to what I can do on the relationship issue if James has no involvement in Morag's therapy. However, in true REBT fashion, his involvement is desirable, but not absolutely necessary!

Criteria for successful outcome

What constitutes 'success' in this case and how is this to be measured? In the past, I used one of a number of belief questionnaires to determine the extent to which clients changed their irrational beliefs to rational beliefs as a result of therapy. I no longer do this, since I believe that any changes are as much a consequence of clients knowing 'the right answer' than of a real therapeutic shift. What I do now is to develop a list of problems and goals and have clients provide regular ratings on a simple 10-point scale. So, what I will probably do with Morag is to encourage her to rate at several points in the therapeutic process:

• the severity of her problems (from 10 = extremely severe to 0 = problem absent);
• the degree of progress she considers that she is making towards her goals (from 0 = no progress to 10 = very great progress); and
• the extent to which she is using the methods she has learned in therapy (from 0 = not at all to 10 = a great deal).

It is difficult to quantify success in any given case, and I do not know what this will mean for Morag until our work is well underway. However, I believe I have made clear what constitutes progress and how I will measure it.

You will by now be clear that I have found this task difficult. There are just too many unknowns to speculate accurately on what Morag's concerns truly are, how I will work with her and how she will respond to that work. While I think Morag will have a relatively good outcome, since she is well motivated, psychologically healthy and ready to make changes in her life, I may be completely wrong. In the words of my friend and colleague, Arnold Lazarus, 'It depends . . .'

Postscript

Throughout this task, I have experienced the therapeutic equivalent of shadow boxing. It is difficult enough to make accurate predictions about our work with clients when we know them and have worked with them. To do so under the present conditions is almost hazardous. So, I close with a warning to you, dear reader: Take everything that I and other contributors have said about Morag and our work with her with a bucket of salt!

Further reading

Bordin, E.S. (1979). The generalizability of the psychoanalytic concept of the working alliance. *Psychotherapy: Theory, Research and Practice,* Vol. 16, pp. 252–60.

Dryden, W. (1991). *Reason and Therapeutic Change.* London: Whurr Publishers.

Dryden, W. and DiGiuseppe, R. (1990). *A Primer on Rational-emotive Therapy.* Champaign, IL: Research Press.

Lazarus, A.A. (1989). *The Practice of Multimodal Therapy,* revised edition. Baltimore, MD: Johns Hopkins University Press.

Lazarus, A.A. and Lazarus, C.N. (1991). *Multimodal Life History Inventory.* Champaign, IL: Research Press.

Weldon, F. (1994). *Affliction.* London: Harper Collins.

PAUL HOLMES

6

PSYCHODRAMA

The therapist

The editors originally asked Michael Watson to write this chapter. However, Mike's untimely and unexpected death in January 1994 (just a few days before the editors undertook the further exploration of Morag's life that had been suggested by him) means that he was unable to complete the task. We are therefore deprived of his ideas and creativity which would have been expressed here.

Mike and I were colleagues and very good friends. Both of us were immersed in the life and politics of the British Psychodrama Association. Mike succeeded me as Chair of the Association, a post he held for four years. It has been an honour (albeit a painful one) to take on the task of completing this chapter in his memory.

Our history as psychodramatists ran in parallel. We first met at the Holwell Centre in Devon in the early 1980s during our training there with Marcia Karp and Ken Sprague. Mike came into the world of psychotherapy through running groups, while teaching in an adolescent psychiatric unit. As a child psychiatrist, I too have run psychodrama groups with adolescents. In the year before his short illness, Mike and I shared the responsibility for writing the editorial commentaries in the book *Psychodrama Since Moreno* (Holmes *et al.* 1994). At his death Mike was in post as the first full-time psychodrama psychotherapist in the National Health Service (NHS). He had also established, with colleagues, a psychotherapy training programme in Stoke-on-Trent, which involved extensive use of, and training in, psychodrama.

I know there were differences in our style, both as therapists and authors. Sadly, I alone must take the responsibility for the content of this chapter, as it has not been possible to follow through in detail any of Mike's thoughts and ideas about this patient. However, I have used his words to introduce the use of the social atom test. Thereafter, I have had to complete the task in my own way.

My style of psychodrama is derived from 'classical' methods of this form of therapy as created by J.L. Moreno and Zerka Moreno. By this I mean that in a session I usually focus on only one member of the group (the 'protagonist') and use the techniques of psychodrama to explore and resolve the dynamics within the group. However, my theoretical understanding of the psychological processes involved in the individual and in the group integrate the original existential roots of psychodrama (Marineau 1989; Holmes *et al.* 1994) with ideas derived from modern object relations (Holmes 1992) and systems theories. Such an integration is perhaps inevitable given my training as an individual psychoanalytic psychotherapist and as a family therapist – modes of treatment I continue to use in my work as a consultant child and adolescent psychiatrist in the NHS.

I have come to see how my style of interaction with the members of a psychodrama group used to be determined by the philosophy, rules and boundaries established by psychoanalysis and by the medical model. While I used the techniques of psychodrama, I did not fully endorse the basic philosophical consequences of psychodrama's existential roots in the 'encounter' between two equals. I remained the rather aloof, distant therapist (or doctor). I am at present exploring, in my clinical practice, the complex issues that result, in the context of psychodrama psychotherapy, of being present both as a 'real, available person' and as a psychotherapist.

Further information requested

Mike Watson suggested to the book's editors that they help Morag dramatically create her social atom as an exploratory exercise. Its use reflects psychodrama's concerns with relationships in its attempts to explore an individual's psychology and personal distress. The concept of the social atom was devised by J.L. Moreno, who said that it could be looked at:

> ... from two directions, from the individual towards the community and from the community towards the individual. In the first case, the 'individual-centered' social atom, one can see how the feelings radiate from him in many directions towards individuals who respond to him by likes, dislikes or indifferences and of whom he is aware, or who choose, reject or are neutral towards him.
>
> (Moreno 1953: 294)

Mike Watson's detailed instructions to the editors started:

Moreno wrote that humans are born into a 'social atom', a social network which continues to affect them throughout life. He believed that the personality of the child evolves from relationships with parents and other important persons with whom there is intimate contact. Social atoms are therefore diagnostic tests, bringing to the surface patterns of relationships and feelings connected with them. The feeling that correlates two or more individuals he called *Tele*. The social atom is therefore a compound of the tele relationships of an individual. As positively or negatively charged persons may leave the individual's social atom and others may enter it, the social atom has an everchanging constellation, but also a basic structure that reflects the client's psychic reality . . .

The client is introduced to the idea that they are going to do an exercise that will reflect how they feel about the important people in their life. They are asked to include all the significant people in their life, family, relations, friends, even pets (which are very often significant others!). They are asked to include anyone they think is significant either in a positive or negative way. They are also asked to include people who may no longer be in physical contact, either because they have died or moved away: they may still be significant and there may be still an internal relationship with that person even though they are no longer present.

The following account is a shortened and edited version of the full record of the social atom exercise conducted with Morag by the series editors. The therapist in this exercise (M.W.) is called the 'director', as psychodrama uses the language of the theatre. M.J. recorded the position of the chairs and the content of the exercise:

The room in which the exercise is carried out has a group of small stackable plastic chairs in the centre, with a number of more solid chairs, some with and some without arms, on the periphery. The director explains that important people in Morag's life are to be represented by different chairs. She chooses to use, rather to the director's surprise, all the chairs in the room, because their variation in size, weight and colour seem to Morag to symbolize different qualities of individuals' relationships with her.

The director indicates a stackable chair in the middle of the room and says, 'That's you'. Morag's placing of chairs (after thinking about a person) is determined and definite. However, she soon realizes she does not think of anyone being behind her, and to make room for the distance of her father and others, she moves her chair back towards the wall. Later she changes her mind, indicating that there are in fact women friends who are ranged like 'an arc around me' behind her, supporting her. She also later moves her father's chair back further away from her; and the position of her brother's chair, in relationship to the chair representing herself, is unclear for a while.

Morag starts by placing her daughter Jessica's chair on its back, slightly under her own chair: 'I want to get this chair very close to me, but sort of under my protection, so I'm going to put it so that it's here'. Morag probably wishes Jessica's chair to be smaller, as she places it tucked partly under her own.

Next, she wants to place the chair for her partner, James, saying, 'I think I want to use the weight of the chairs to indicate pressure from them. This one is like half-way between the heavy and the lighter ones – a half-way chair – because it gives me both. It gives me pleasure and, you know, light feelings, but it also gives me some heavy feelings as well'.

Morag then chooses a slightly heavier chair for her mother, which she places quite near her and her daughter and further from James. She uses the stackable chairs again to represent her stepchildren: 'My inclination is to use a lighter chair because although they do cause me anxiety they are actually young, therefore it's kind of, that's sort of, not exactly that they're not responsible, but they're . . . James's son is nearest James – he's proud of all his children, but I think he takes a particular delight in John. This seems OK for Debbie as well'.

Debbie's chair is placed face-to-face with Morag's; John's at more of an angle: 'Because the chair is facing this way, because people are relating to me. I can't see there are many people behind me'. So at this point she moves all the chairs she has so far placed back a yard and a half.

'My father'. She thinks about this for a while. 'Well I might change this . . . it might need to go further away . . . because he's further away . . . he brings with him some responsibilities but because he's further away, if you like, they are smaller. If he lived right next door he might be more . . . Now this is Carl, the chap that I used to go out with. And I've picked an armchair because I still see him in a supporting role, if you like, but obviously not nearly as big as that'.

She places another chair next to her father's: 'My younger sister. My older sister – I would probably go for one of those chairs'. She indicates a chair like James's. 'It's to do with burden and responsibility. It's, you know . . . it brings pleasure but it also brings the feeling that they're going to need help and support probably'.

At this point, Morag moves her father's chair back a bit, further away from her. 'Now my brother . . . I want my brother to be close to my mother, nearer my mother, but heavier. This is a person that makes me sigh when I think of him and his entourage'. She places the chair on top of the Carl chair and then continues to talk about her brother.

The director then says, 'Anybody else you'd like to include?' Morag replies: 'Well possibly, well, I didn't really know my grandparents, but possibly put my uncle, who was my mother's brother, over there somewhere. Yes that's OK. I think it's really a question of where you stop. I do have other friends that are important to me – that do enter the picture'.

The director says, 'Any particular friends?' Morag replies: 'Again these really need to be sort of armchair types, but not as big as my mother's armchairs – you know, little armchairs. This is a woman (later identified as Hannah) that I opened my business with, who is very, very, supportive. She's gone on to be something different, but she's very, very close, close to me . . . um . . .'.

The director invites her to look around, to check it and see if she wants to alter anything, to move anything around. She says: 'How do you feel at this point?' Morag points behind her saying, 'Um . . . I feel . . . kind of . . . yes . . . I feel kind of comforted by those ones'. It becomes clear that in Morag's mind there is an imaginary 'arc' of chairs around the back of her own chair representing a number of supportive women friends: 'I think it's good. I think it is interesting that I have arranged them in a kind of arc around me, you know, kind of that's my support'.

> *Director*: Supposing you sit in the chair that's you, and get a sense of how it feels then, see if there's anything you want to move then.
>
> *Morag*: I'd like a smaller chair for my daughter.
>
> *Director*: You want to encompass it a bit?
>
> *Morag*: Yes. James is definitely right, close to me, but he's half and half, he's half supporting, but he's half demanding . . . It's difficult to get John in the right position probably because he oscillates, sometimes I think he is . . . and at other times, he's . . . you know. My father . . . yes father's right to be a bigger burden. Yeah.

The director now explains to her that she can sit in any chair and for a moment, as she wishes, can become that person. She suggests that Morag can take on their persona – and say something they would say as that person, either about themselves or what they might say to Morag. She thinks for a while and then moves into James's chair. When she sits down she says, 'It's not so easy when you sit down in a chair as when you are looking at the chair. I guess he would say that . . .'.

The director asks her to use the first person. Morag then speaks as James: '"There is conflict in my life between what I think I would like to be doing and the job that I am doing. I feel a great burden of responsibility in the job that I'm doing, not only to my boss, who put me in this situation, but also to the people who work in the company. But in my heart of hearts I would like to be a photographer"'.

The director invites her to repeat this with any of the other people in her life. Morag thinks where to move next, before moving to her friend Hannah's chair. 'This friend here is called Hannah . . . "I think Morag is her own worst enemy. Always rushing around, doing far too much, but that's part of, that's part of her"'.

Morag moves to her mother's chair: 'My mother. "I love my daughter very much. I wish she would spend more time with me. I'm proud of what she does. I don't think that James is the right person for her. I think he's too moody . . . I wish she'd spend more time with me"'.

Morag thinks for a long time before she decides to sit in her brother's chair, from which she describes his perceptions of his confusions in life. She then moves on to Debbie's and John's chairs: 'Debbie. "I wish people would cuddle me a bit more. I have the feeling that I'm perhaps . . . a bit of a nuisance to everybody . . . I enjoy being with my friends, so I don't get that impression from my friends . . . "'.

'I'm now John. "Things are OK. I enjoy playing sport, being successful at sport. I'm, I'm quite happy to . . . um . . . to play people to get the best advantage for me. If I can't get what I want from . . . one supporting person, I'll go back and try somebody and try a different person . . . I'll always be all right anyway because grandma and grandpa will always get me what I want"'.

Morag thinks some more and then says, 'That's about it'.

The director invites Morag to sit back in her own chair and asks her to look around and see whether she wants to reposition any of the chairs. She then asks her to move any chairs in her social atom into a position that, if she got a special wish, she would rather see them in. Morag thinks about this for a long while, murmurs the task to herself, and thinks again.

'I was thinking whether I would like James to change totally into one of the armchairs, but on reflection I don't think I would because, er, I think . . . James if you like has got to be an equal. He's not got to be totally supporting . . . I think the only one I would change is, I would like it if my brother . . . changed from a heavy black chair into a supporting chair and came closer to my mother'. She moves his chair so that it lies close to her mother's. The director then asks: 'What would have to happen for your brother to change position?' Morag replies: 'Um . . . I think he would need to rethink the whole of his life [*a little laugh*]. If his attitude to his job changed so that he could get it in perspective I guess, so that he could spend much more time with his wife and family, which would make them happier, which would make them not so jealous of any attention he paid to my mother . . . you know, if just . . . his . . . if he could get things in perspective more, and not spend sort of hours doing things he shouldn't be doing, less workaholic, more balanced person, who would then have more time, to give a bit more, you know, love and support to my mother, which I feel would make her happier and would it – possibly it, it would relieve the burden on me . . . a bit. It would make her . . . I think it would make him happier too, if he sorted out the rest of his life, sort of thing'.

Director: Is this the only one you want to change?
Morag: Yes. I feel that's interesting because I should . . .
          maybe I should want John and Debbie to get closer
          to them, but I don't know.
Director: You should?
Morag: Yes, the feeling I have is that if any of these ones
          came any closer to me they would bring the burden
          closer to me as well.

Morag's initial session raised several questions in my mind about her relationships with her family. The structured nature of the social atom test, and the directive role of the facilitator, 'contains' (in the psychoanalytic sense) some of Morag's anxieties. As a consequence, Morag is able to provide more information about her family during the externalization of her social atom than she had been in the first, less structured, meeting.

Seeing Morag construct her social atom provides me with at least partial answers to my questions, as the use of this technique allows us to develop more understanding of the intra-psychic roots of Morag's discontent. For example, it appears that she does indeed have a rather ambivalent relationship with her father, whom she sees as a pressure in her life (albeit one that exists at a distance). Her stepchildren, too, are perceived as potential burdens: if she allows them to become closer to her, she may grow to resent them more. However, it is apparent that her relationship with her mother is positive and close, if 'enveloping', as is Morag's relationship with her own daughter whom she feels she 'encompasses'.

Assessment

Morag arrived late for the initial appointment and thereafter filled the session with information about certain aspects of her life with little prompting. By her own account, she is a woman in a rush, always moving onwards and forwards towards new ventures, goals and relationships. She is hard-working, organized and has achieved a great deal in her life. However, at times, she feels rather confused and dissatisfied. While early in the session she described two areas of her life with which she would like help, a feature of her session was how little she actually spoke about herself. In many ways, she seems more at ease talking about her husband, his children and their mother (her husband's ex-wife), and one of her own former partners. Morag spontaneously gave a lot of information about herself. However, there was no mention of her own family of origin, a total absence that seems rather strange to me.

According to Peter Felix Kellermann (pers. comm.), who trained in New York with Moreno, 'it is rare for psychodramatists to make preliminary intake interviews, engage in history taking and administer psychological tests prior to treatment. The information revealed by such evaluations, they say, better serves the needs of the therapist than it does the client because, whatever information needed by the protagonist will anyway be revealed during the psychodramatic action' (see also Kellermann 1992). I must add that Kellermann himself seriously questions this position.

I always meet with people who wish to join my weekly psychodrama therapy group, for an hour or so, to talk about why they want help. However, I do not normally undertake detailed, in-depth psychological assessments of those seeking treatment with me. I go with the flow and energy of the person's wish for help. The three most important aspects of my decision-making process, when interviewing people for a psychodrama group, are:

1 Their own views on why they are seeking help.
2 My own emotional reaction to them.
3 The presence or absence of what might be called 'exclusion' criteria.

First, Morag has very clear ideas as to why she wishes to become involved in psychotherapy. Within a few minutes of the start of the meeting, she has clearly described two areas of concern: her relationship with her partner's teenage children and her wish to talk about and understand 'why I enjoy doing things'. However, as she continued to talk, a third problem became apparent; namely, her feelings for her former partner, Carl.

The psychotherapeutic method of psychodrama encourages participants (or patients) to take a significant degree of control in their own therapeutic destiny. In therapy and in any particular session, the process starts with some sort of contract being made between the director (the psychodrama psychotherapist) and the protagonist as to 'what I need (or want) to work on now'. The therapeutic agenda is set by the client rather than the therapist. Some psychodramatists make this contact explicit ('so in this session we are going to work on the row you had at work today'), whereas others are somewhat less overt.

Morag's clear statements of problems (albeit that the second of the three has a rather diffuse existential quality) bode well for her involvement in psychodrama. They provide sufficient information for there to be the basis of a therapeutic contract between Morag and myself.

Second, I need also to be keenly aware of my own response to Morag. Do I feel positive towards her? I must also try to sense how she feels towards me. J.L. Moreno used the term *tele* to describe the reciprocal feelings (which may be positive or negative) that develop between people. In Moreno's view, *tele* is not determined by an individual's past experiences, but is an unconscious communication of aspects on oneself (see Blatner, in Holmes *et al.* 1994). I feel on the whole positive towards Morag and feel that we could work together on any issues that emerged in the group.

The third criterion for my believing someone might benefit in psychodrama is the absence of factors that might disrupt their work in the group, such as any tendencies to act out (in a very destructive way), or to abuse drugs or alcohol, or to slip into psychosis. Problems in these areas would, at least in my private practice, be clear indications to be cautious about offering treatment (Holmes 1995). If I feel that someone is avoiding issues that might lead me to exclude them from a group, I will also ask specific questions about their past life and present circumstances, slipping into my psychiatric mode of history taking.

While Morag talked about her life, she provided answers to some of the questions that were going through my mind. She gave no hint of factors that might make me consider excluding her from my group. Indeed, she described many signs of her strengths: she was in work, was able to maintain good relationships with friends, and reasonable ones with her sexual partners. She was curious about herself and self-questioning.

I have a particular interest in the style and nature of the relationships people have with others (and indeed with internal aspects of themselves). I look for information which will give me some insights into their psychological inner world of internalized early relationships, relationships which still exert a powerful influence on their life. My existential approach to providing psychodramatic therapy does not stop me making my own observations about someone (which I may not share with them at first), and asking myself questions that may not be answered until after many months of therapy. I use all the information I have about an individual (including my own response to them) to develop hypotheses about what makes them 'tick'.

I believe that a crucial aspect of psychotherapy is the creation, by the patient with the assistance of their therapist, of a psychic map which links together their past, present and future. Throughout therapy, as my part in this process, I am looking for landmarks, directions and links that will in time furnish details of this map. The monitoring, in an assessment, of what I sense to be clinically important facts and observations, leads me to questions and hypotheses that are part of my map-making process. The following are some of the facts, observations, questions and hypotheses raised in my mind during Morag's initial session:

Some facts
- She gets angry with her stepchildren.
- She lives with partners for six or seven years, then moves on to another relationship.
- She is frustrated by her partner's lack of fulfilment in his job.
- She maintains a separate part of the house for herself and her daughter from which her partner is excluded.
- Her partner blames his ex-wife's therapy for the break-up of their marriage.
- When she discovered that her former partner Carl had no plans to marry her, Morag went out and found another man (her present partner), with whom she became involved after a fairly short period of time.

Some observations
- She often never reaches the 'punch line' of many of her sentences, changing the topic part way through.
- She appears somewhat preoccupied by her own reactions to her partner's ex-wife's behaviour.
- She describes the issue of free choice, 'having *carte blanche* to do what you want', as a problem, since you then 'can't think about what you do want'.

- Her eyes water when she says (referring to James), 'I'm fairly determined that I want this relationship to stay. You know, to grow old together'.
- She gets upset talking about Carl: 'maybe I should do a bit of exorcism on the Carl time'.
- Morag appears to have a positive caring relationship with her daughter.

Some questions
- Why is she so upset by her aggressive response to selfish teenagers?
- Why, when she appears to resent looking after these children and feeding her partner, has she created her own mobile catering business?
- Why does she make no reference to any members of her family of origin?

Three hypotheses
1 Morag's high levels of anxiety stop her finishing some of her sentences. She thereby avoids the open and public statement of potentially contentious or distressing issues that were, perhaps, going to form the second part of her unfinished sentences. Her behaviour may be a form of intra-psychic and interpersonal conflict avoidance.
2 The real roots of Morag's request for therapy lie in her ambivalent relationship with her partner James, and her unresolved feelings about her former partner Carl.
3 Morag makes no reference in her initial assessment interview to any members of her family of origin. It may be that her problems with maintaining intimate relationships with men derive from difficulties in her relationship with her own parents, perhaps in particular with her father.

No doubt once Morag enters therapy, the links will become clearer. The facts and observations and their relative importance will be revised, some of the questions answered and the hypotheses 'tested', all at a pace and a depth to be determined by Morag. To quote Zerka Moreno in a personal communication, 'I only really get to know someone once I have seen their psychodrama'.

On the basis of this initial meeting, I feel positive towards Morag. She has described a clear wish to 'work on herself' in therapy. She has also told me nothing about herself which would lead me to exclude her from a group. I feel able to offer Morag a place in my weekly psychodrama therapy group.

Therapeutic possibilities

As I have indicated above, I believe that Morag could benefit from a psychodrama group. I now consider some of the factors that lead me to this conclusion.

While the ability to 'think psychologically about oneself' is not an essential prerequisite for therapy, I think its presence helps, at least in the early stages of treatment. Morag certainly shows curiosity about herself and the possible causes of her confusions. I have suggested that her tendency not to finish certain sentences suggests a degree of intra-psychic (and perhaps interpersonal) conflict avoidance. While this aspect of her personality in no way precludes her gaining benefit from a psychodrama group, I predict that it would need addressing if Morag was not to just 'go round in circles' in therapy, thereby avoiding any real resolution to her conflicts.

The therapeutic process in psychodrama works in an incremental manner, in as much as in any session usually only one issue or dilemma is addressed for one member of the group. The others take roles in the protagonist's psychodrama; for example, in Morag's case, the focus might be 'confronting my stepchildren', or 'the things I've never said to Carl'.

Behind each of these issues there of course lie other problems and conflicts. Indeed, the very power of these problems to distress Morag suggests that they may, in part, reflect repetitions of relationships from her past (say her own early childhood and adolescence), which now form part of her own psychic inner world. Morag has an ability to define areas of distress and conflict, any one of which would make suitable starting points for a psychodrama.

Psychodrama, although it can be used with a single patient and empty chairs, is usually considered to be a form of group psychotherapy (a term coined by J.L. Moreno in 1932). Morag's account of her life, and relatively long-term, stable relationships with a variety of people, suggests that she would be able to work on her problems in a group. It is very important that individuals starting therapy in a group have the willingness and strength to work on their problems in such a setting. Although a session may focus on one person and one issue, it must be stressed that in on-going therapy the group dynamics and complex interpersonal relationships of group members are also of the greatest importance. In their own way, they provide the material for psychodramatic explorations. These interactions also have the potential to provide both support and stress to group members. Individuals with significant issues about dependency, or those with a tendency to destructive acting-out, may find the psychological containment provided by the therapist and the group insufficient to their needs. Such people may do better, at least in the early stages of their treatment, in one-to-one psychotherapy. Morag, by her own account, leads a very busy and perhaps rather over-committed life. I have some concern that the various pressures (which she talks about as burdens) might make regular attendance at the group difficult. This is therefore a possible reservation about Morag's potential to do well in psychodrama.

The course of therapy

Following my initial meeting with Morag, and my decision that she might benefit from psychodrama, 1 would need to decide what sort of group to offer, since I run both psychodrama weekend workshops and slow-open, on-going weekly psychotherapy groups.

A weekend workshop

I often suggest to people seeking psychotherapy with me, who know nothing about psychodrama (or indeed about me), that they might first attend a weekend workshop. Such two-day events usually have groups of between eight to twelve people, at least five of whom become protagonists in full psychodrama or shorter vignettes.

Joining a weekend workshop might be a very good next step for Morag. She has been able to define her areas of difficulty, but there is no real sense of great urgency. Whilst waiting to start psychotherapy, she knows nothing about psychodrama or me, so a weekend together would also allow for a much more detailed period of mutual appraisal. Moreover, her general coping skills (demonstrated by her lifestyle and personal history) suggest that she would be able to handle this style of slow entry into therapy. Indeed, such a process might increase her commitment should she finally decide to join a weekly therapy group.

Psychodrama can be considered to be a therapy of relationships. The therapeutic process entails creating dialogues between people (played by the protagonist and other members of the group) on the psychodramatic stage. These are often representations of real individuals who are – or who have been – in relationship with the protagonist, such as father or mother, husband or wife. At other times, and perhaps more especially with more 'schizoid' personalities, these dialogues have a tendency to develop between different parts of the self; for example, the 'angry inner self' in confrontation with the 'inner child self'.

In my experience, a single weekend can provide some participants with significant therapeutic benefits. This is perhaps because the nature of psychodrama involves focusing on specific problems or relationships (in order to create clarity in the drama). This allows for the exploration and perhaps resolution of these issues (see Holmes 1992). However, I always make it clear to those attending a workshop that my contract with them is to offer an experience of psychodrama, not psychotherapy. I am aware that while mutative events may occur for some people, others will emerge from the weekend, as might be expected, unmoved and unchanged.

Morag clearly describes a number of focal problems, most of which are connected with her relationships in the present: with her partner James, his children and ex-wife, and her former partner. Her ability to define areas of distress or conflict bodes well for her ability to benefit from psychodrama. Indeed, some of her problems might be very powerfully and successfully addressed in the context of a 'one-off' weekend psychodrama workshop, during which she might, for example, choose to work on her relationship with her stepchildren. The social atom test might be used as a warm-up to psychotherapeutic work within the group. While enacting her social atom, Morag (in role reversal, 'being' John) said: 'If I can't get what I want from . . . one supporting person I'll go back and try someone else . . . John's always like that, so self-centred sometimes I could . . .'.

As always, her words trail off. As the psychodrama director I would now move her from words to action. Here I move from Morag's actual words into a hypothetical example of what my dramatic interventions might be:

Director: OK, Morag, don't tell us, show us what happened.
Describe the kitchen to us, and lay it out in this room using the chairs and cushions. Thank you.
Now reverse roles and be John for a moment. OK.
John, tell us a bit about yourself. How old are you? How do you get on with Morag?

Morag: [speaking as John]: Well, I'm fifteen, and doing my GCSE exams. But this morning I'm off to play football, so I need my breakfast; and Morag's being so slow. I'll miss the bus.

Director: OK. Thank you John. Reverse Morag: be yourself again. Now, who in the group could play John for you?

Morag: Stan.

Director: OK Stan: could you be John, sitting in his chair, and repeat those words?

Morag: [At this point she becomes very angry] I'm not your

slave! You sit there and demand your breakfast. If I
were your mother I'd throw you out of the house!
Director: What stops you now?
Morag: I couldn't because . . . that . . . because it would upset
James . . .

And so the session might continue with other members of the group
being asked to play Debbie, James, and so on as required by the
drama. But psychodrama is much more than the mere repetition of
life and the action could now move in at least two directions.

For example, it could be used, in a form of *role rehearsal*, to allow
Morag to say important things to the children that normal conven-
tions in her family, and her own tendency to avoid conflict, forbid.
Voicing unspoken thoughts in the safety of the group can be very
therapeutic. Furthermore, Morag might feel empowered to go home
and try saying the same things in reality!

Alternatively, the potential roots of Morag's difficulties with these
teenagers might be explored through scenes that take her back to
her own childhood, and her relationships with her parents and
siblings. Goldman and Morrison (1984) describe the structure of a
psychodrama session as a spiral, in which a series of dramatic scenes
or episodes are explored in turn, each one further back in time. All
the scenes have psychological and symbolic links for the protagonist.

Morag's psychodrama could have started with her confrontation
with her stepchildren. Through this scene, the failure of the teenagers' father to play his role in controlling their behaviour (and thereby
putting more pressure on Morag) might emerge as an issue. This in
turn could lead to a scene in which the teenage Morag confronts her
father for his own distance from her and the day-to-day life of their
family. The insight that could develop from this scene might then
help Morag understand some of her current frustrations with her
partner James, issues she might then take up with him when she
returns home.

After a single psychodrama, I would expect Morag to be able to
address some of the issues with those she lives with. Many other
issues would, of course, not be touched upon. Such therapy in a
short workshop might be said to bring about first-degree change (i.e.
of behaviour in one relationship), but not second-degree change
(i.e. at more depth in the psyche, involving aspects of the protagonist's personality).

The weekly psychodrama group

Following a weekend workshop, Morag might decide to join an ongoing group meeting once a week for two and half hours. It would

have seven or eight members, who have been in the group for up to three years. Such a group also uses the methods of protagonist-centred psychodrama (each week one person is the focus of the group's work). But the fact that people meet together week by week alters the dynamics of the group process. Relationships develop between group members, and between each person and the director (therapist), which become deeper and more trusting. However, at times these relationships are influenced by the group members' own past experiences. Issues around sibling rivalry are stirred up, as are old styles of relating to parents. These types of reaction are determined by each individual's inner world. Group analysts would called these 'transference' responses. The time and space available in such a group allows each individual, over a period of months, to explore and re-explore (often from different perspectives), his or her conflicts, distress and dilemmas. Each person's private therapeutic journey nevertheless influences everyone else in the group.

My approach to psychodrama links the classical methods of Moreno with a model of intra-psychic function based on object relations theory. In on-going weekly therapy, I will seek to make the links between Morag's present relationships and those in her childhood. In her assessment interviews, Morag did not even mention her family of origin, although the subsequent social atom exercise added information about this area of her life. My theoretical position suggests the current difficulties in her relationships are often underpinned, and indeed at times driven, by unresolved issues from the past. I would expect that in the group some of the links would begin to surface for Morag, allowing her both to make cognitive sense of her psychic map, and to experience the catharsis of (for example) her rage with her father.

Problem areas

Morag's tendency to avoid the emotional point and to slip sideways in certain conflictual situations might present a potential problem in her therapy. As I have already indicated, I see a link between her habit of not finishing sentences and her emotionally unresolved relationship with Carl. When it comes to the emotional crunch, Morag might resist the therapeutic process.

Moreno, however, talks about 'going with the resistance' (rather than going *for* it through interpretation, as in psychoanalysis). As her psychodrama director I will go with the flow, trusting that Morag's own wish for resolution will be a drive for therapeutic progress. At worst, Morag may begin to use the pressure of her family and two part-time jobs as an excuse to miss sessions. If this happens, her behaviour will need to be addressed directly in the sessions.

Another area of potential difficulty relates to what I presume to be ambivalent feelings towards her father. It is possible that (if I am on the right lines) Morag may develop a complex relationship with me, that is to an extent determined by her childhood relationship with her father. These transferential feelings towards me, should they become very negative or eroticized, might become disruptive in the group.

Whenever possible I try to tackle any difficulties in group members' relationships with me through the use of psychodramatic methods, rather than through the use of analytic interpretations. For example, should Morag appear very angry with me in one session, for no apparent logical reason, I will ask her to address an empty chair representing myself. This technique allows me to regain my adult-to-adult working relationship with her, while allowing her to express her feelings to me. I may ask her to role reverse with me (i.e. to sit in 'my' chair) and respond, as me, to her own comments addressed to me. At times in such a process I may get the feeling that Morag is speaking as if she is no longer an adult. I may then prompt her by saying, 'How old do you feel now?', or 'Have you felt like this before?'. 'Oh yes', she may reply, 'I feel that I'm now eight, when my father left home for the first time'. This technique allows links to be made between the present and the past, as the psychodrama moves into scenes (in this example with her father) from her adolescence or childhood.

Sometimes group members may have reality-based complaints to make against me as the director and a member of the group. These should always be addressed directly, in a person-to-person encounter, before they are redirected into any psychodramatic exploration. To ignore reality in favour of the transference and the past is an abuse of the therapeutic technique.

Criteria for successful outcome

I believe that all of us continue to develop and change psychologically and socially from birth to death. A period of time in psychotherapy, be it a weekend psychodrama workshop or ten years in psychoanalysis, is but a step on this journey. I never look for complete success in any therapy. All I hope for is that my patients know themselves better, and feel more at ease in their relationships with the world. For some people, therapy brings about amazing changes and resolutions of conflict; for others, it enables a slightly better adjustment to the world, and greater stability is all that can be expected.

Morag's progress in therapy can be viewed from at least two perspectives: hers and mine. For Morag, progress will be achieved if her overt causes of distress (e.g. her feelings about her stepchildren, and about James and Carl) are eased. I would also see any such reductions in her 'symptoms' as good therapeutic progress. However, I am also interested in seeing her develop an understanding of the links between her past, her psychic inner world and her present behaviour.

Perhaps, in the end, Morag will be the best judge of progress, as she was the one who in the first place went looking for help.

Summary

Working in a psychodrama group is rather like being a member of a precision ballroom dancing team which, sometimes without warning, has to change its dance tempo from a slow waltz to a torrid rumba as material from all our inner worlds bubbles to the surface.

The philosophy of the method requires me to develop an open and authentic relationship with all the members of the group, which at times will be reciprocated. But then, with little warning, deep-seated and ancient aspects of an individual's inner world can begin to dominate the process and I can be seen as, say, their angry or abusive mother. With care and tact I must redirect this energy into a psychodramatic exploration of this relationship: their mother is then played by another member of the group. The more I practise psychodrama in weekly therapy groups, the more excited I have become with its potential to explore the deepest aspects of the human mind, in the context of open and responsive relationships between group members. As the process of therapy progresses, I have no doubt that I and Morag and the other members of the group will learn to perfect our psychic dancing skills.

Dedication

This chapter is dedicated to Michael Watson.

Further reading

Goldman, E.E. and Morrison, D.S. (1984). *Psychodrama*. Phoenix, Arizona: Kendall-Hunt.

Holmes, P. (1992). *The Inner World Outside: Object Relations Theory and Psychodrama*. London: Tavistock/Routledge.

Holmes, P. (1995). 'Would you like a cup of tea or coffee?': Assessment for psychodrama. In C. Mace (ed.), *The Art and Science of Psychotherapy Assessment*. London: Tavistock/Routledge.

Holmes, P., Karp, M. and Watson, M. (eds) (1994). *Psychodrama Since Moreno: Innovations in Theory and Practice*. London: Tavistock/Routledge.

Kellermann, P.F. (1992). *Focus on Psychodrama: The Therapeutic Aspects of Psychodrama*. London: Jessica Kingsley.

Marineau, R.F. (1989). *Jacob Levy Moreno 1889-1974: Father of Psychodrama, Sociometry and Group Psychotherapy*. London: Tavistock/Routledge.

Moreno, J.L. (1953). *Who Shall Survive? Foundations of Sociometry, Group Psychotherapy and Sociodrama*. Beacon, NY: Beacon House Inc.

ARTHUR JONATHAN

EXISTENTIAL PSYCHOTHERAPY

The therapist

I received my training as a psychotherapist in the School of Psycho-therapy and Counselling of Regent's College, London where I gained an MA Degree in Psychotherapy and Counselling and, subsequently, the Advanced Diploma in Existential Psychotherapy. I am an existential psychotherapist working in private practice with both individuals and couples.

My approach to working with clients centres on the client being-in-the-world as expressed by the client's disclosure of their on-going relations with the world. The therapy is therefore concerned with the exploration and clarification of the various relational aspects of the client's existence that define and provide meaning for them at all levels of their existence. I would try to facilitate a process whereby these relational orientations may be clarified and confronted in ways that promote an attitude of openness to the possibilities of human existence. The requirement is for me to attend to the client's experience of being-in-the-world. Then, through descriptively focused interpretations, I can attempt to clarify the client's meaning-world with them. This provides the client with the experience of being heard, and hearing themselves, in a manner that is both non-judgemental and accepting of the stance they maintain. In order for this to take place, however, the process challenges me, as the therapist, to consider and confront the biases and assumptions that I bring to the encounter and which will impede my ability to listen openly and respectfully to the client's communications. In other words, I would need to suspend, as far as I am able, my own biases, presuppositions, beliefs and prejudices, in order to allow an openness to the client's experiences and to be thus better able to listen, hear and attend to the client.

My approach is primarily one of descriptive analysis emerging from an engagement in dialogue with the client wherein clarification and challenge can take place. The engagement is close, earnest and open and quite different from the adoption of a more remote or instructional stance focused upon causally derived diagnosis and symptom removal. I would not be influencing or driving the client towards any preconceived goal or outcome: it is the process which is important. The meeting between myself and the client is therefore regarded as a central enterprise, because it is through this relationship that the client's issues are manifested and opened up to examination and exploration. The approach does not depend upon a specific set of techniques or 'doing' skills, but rather emphasizes the personal qualities of the therapist and the notion of 'relation' and encounter in the therapeutic process.

Within this encounter, I can encourage the client to slow down and examine and explore issues more closely; to challenge the sedimented assumptions and beliefs of the client; and to assist the client in the consideration of options, choices and alternative strategies, as well as the results and effects of their decisions.

Further information requested

The ten further questions I asked were designed for exploration and clarification of certain concerns, issues, feelings and understanding relating to Morag herself and to Morag in her relationships.

1 *You say very little that is positive about your relationship with James. You talk about difficulties; there are some criticisms of him and you also speak about his dependence on you. What is it that exists between you that makes the relationship worthwhile? We don't get a sense of what makes it important for it to have to succeed?*
Morag's reply is interspersed with several pauses, one of them quite long. One can only conjecture on what was going on for her here, or what it was that lay behind the pauses. Nevertheless, this for me would enter the realm of additional information. It would be interesting to explore this process that is going on for her. Something is making her hesitate, pause and take time over her response to the question. Her remarks about James in their relationship are almost totally positive, although there are slight qualifications, and these I would also regard as being indicators of further exploratory possibilities. This may be an indication of a problem. There is so much riding on holding on to the relationship that she is both unwilling and unable to truly open up to it in all its problems and difficulties:

we have to face the negatives if we are to get positive results. There is every indication here that there is much more in the relationship that bears looking at more closely. She is presenting as positive a picture as she can, but not succeeding completely. She does not want to paint a thoroughly gloomy portrait of James, since we know from the first interview that she wants very much for this relationship to succeed. Right towards the end of her response she comes to what appears to be the strongest reason for this, something she has already referred to in the first interview and which now re-emerges from among all the reasons she has given. This is the fact that they have had a child, together. For her this has been 'the biggest commitment of them all, and I would never want to break that'. Are there other aspects of the relationship that she needs to examine more closely?

2 *I asked for clarification of her emphasis on the fact that she and James are not married.*
Her response is straightforward and unequivocal: 'I feel strongly that marriage takes away your identity and your individuality, especially for women'. She was married at twenty to a man who 'put me down professionally', felt he was better than she was, when she believed otherwise, and 'just wanted to know when I was going to have children and things like that'. James has occasionally hinted at marriage, but she said: '. . . can't, er . . . I don't want to lose my individuality'. I would like to explore this with her in terms of her present relationship, especially since in her relationship with Carl, which came in between the other two, it was she who wanted to get married and have children. In fact, one of the reasons for leaving Carl was that she believed that he was never going to marry her. These contradictions need some attention and unravelling. Her fear of marriage may be a weakening factor: she is on the defensive, not confident that she can hold her own side up. James as a husband would be a threat, so James must be a threat now too.

3 In her response to my question relating to terminating a pregnancy, Jessica's birth later on and James's feelings at the time, Morag says that there is a question in her mind about whether James used the termination in evidence against her. She also connects it with his not really wanting another child but, once having got her, loving her very much and maybe blaming Morag for putting him through all this trauma. This response appears to direct a lot of blame towards James. It removes any focus from Morag and with it any consideration of her responsibility or involvement. For these reasons, further discussion may prove helpful in order to discover what her own attitude is.

4 *This has to do with your relationship with the children. What comes through is that you feel a sense of distance from them. I was wondering what you are experiencing regarding what is missing in order to achieve greater closeness with them?*
Morag seizes on one phrase ('what is missing') in answering the question and is thus able to limit her response to the fact that they are not her own children – the biological link is missing – and therefore she feels differently towards them and treats them differently. The question as it was phrased was not very helpful in opening up lines of exploration.

5 In response to a question about herself and Paula, Morag talks in disparaging terms about Paula doing 'the helpless female bit' and thus letting the side down. In so doing, she alludes somewhat indirectly to the beliefs and assumptions she (Morag) holds about how a woman should be in a relationship. Pursuing this line of exploration, asking Morag to describe what concept she has of this may be quite helpful in bringing her greater understanding of herself in relationships.

6 My next question had to do with the idea of growing old, as well as growing old with James. I wanted Morag to examine both these notions in terms of what they represented to her. The therapist added a question which, in my opinion, somewhat shifted the focus and concentrated it on the thoughts, feelings and images which came to mind when she thought about growing old with James. Her response is nevertheless very interesting and provides a basis for further examination and discussion. It has both positive and negative aspects to it. On the positive side, she starts to describe her 'ideal world' of a relationship: the sort of relationship she would like to have with James. On the negative side, she describes what breaking up with James would mean to her purely in terms of inconvenience to herself. It seems to me that she is missing something here which could be very important: she only hints at part of it in passing, when she talks about she and James having differences, but nevertheless having a basis on which to build. I would be interested to explore both the differences and commonalities more fully with her. It also seems to me that my original questions, about what growing old and the idea of growing old with James represented to her, still need to be addressed.

7 When asked about a possible conflict between representing herself as one who wants to be open to so many possibilities, change and new things on the one hand, and yet talking about 'should', 'must' and 'have to' on the other, Morag recounts an analogy from

an American tape she has listened to. She acknowledges that there is a conflict and that she would really rather opt for openness and the possibility of change. She does not, however, examine this in any depth, merely making a statement and leaving it at that. I would point this out to her, thereby encouraging further description and exploration. This illustrates that it is not the asking of a particular question that advances the work, but the subtle interplay of client and therapist response and exploration of what emerges.

8 Morag found the question about her own family life and background rather involved, but nevertheless responded with some significant statements. She does feel swamped by the needs of other people, but does not expand further than a statement. There is room here for further exploration. When talking about her own family, she reveals that she was third in a family of four, that her mother was very busy and had to return to full-time work when Morag was six, and that they had au pairs and 'people like that to help' because her father 'was absent a lot of the time, most of the time'. These are obviously things which hold significance for her; yet she does not discuss them in any depth, so that their significance in her present life cannot be estimated or gauged in any way. I would like to consider with her what her experiences have inclined her to expect, or not to expect, from family life.

9 Morag's desires, hopes and aspirations appear limited to three areas, which seem to me to be worthy of more discussion: her desire to get involved in another project; her hopes that Jessica, her daughter, will turn out to be a reasonably happy person; and her further hope that she and James manage to stay together. She adds that she does not really have any clear vision about where she is going. Questions about a notion of there being perhaps a prescribed, ideal way of living one's life with others arise when I remember other things she has said in this regard earlier. I would like to put some of these points to her. It is also interesting to note that she feels no commitment to helping James, but is rather engaged in competing to raise his children: is this not a responsibility she has to some extent taken on?

10 In response to my final question about where she is now, she reveals her concern about James's children and her feelings of guilt about not allowing them to stay with her and James. This response indicates Morag's preoccupation with the previous question! She is worried that her selfishness may have scarred them. The need, it seems to me, is not to push these feelings away, but rather to come

to terms with them and with the situation. This is really important: there is existential guilt here. Morag knows that she is falling short. This is a crucial area for our work together.

Having to pose these additional questions is not a true reflection of the way I work with a client. I would not normally ask so many questions or, for that matter, use a questioning technique. My interventions would normally be in the form of statements, often rather short statements, summarizing, paraphrasing and re-phrasing and sometimes using silent interventions, all designed to open up the possibility of further exploration and examination, rather than closing down the client as questions sometimes do. Part of the problem with posing questions is that they often direct the client towards some specific response or they limit the client in her response. My feeling, when reading her responses to some of my additional questions, is one of frustration in not being there to follow on with further gentle probing, or with some sort of challenge.

Assessment

From the introductory notes and verbatim report of the first session, my early impressions of Morag are of a well-educated person who can verbally present herself very effectively. She is in mid-life, with a partner of almost the same age. When Morag starts speaking, she is quickly into herself, passing swiftly from a short description of the family to a description of her two jobs, especially her own private business. There is a sense that she experiences herself as an independent professional person and that this perhaps overrides her sense of motherhood: 'I work . . . I have my own private business which I started when I had my daughter'. It is in her early remarks that Morag's value and belief system becomes apparent. One firmly held expectation of hers seems to be that society ought to accommodate and cater for women with children in a practical way. Because she has found these expectations of society to be largely unrealistic, she has responded by setting up a private business, withdrawing into her own territory as a strategy, and employing fifteen single-parent staff. It is my impression that she feels an antagonism against a society which does not cater for women in this way, and that the strategy she has adopted is one of trying to lodge a protest against society on the one hand, and trying by direct action to remedy and improve society on the other. This shows great determination and resourcefulness, but also possibly a tendency to fly into action – with a hint of self-righteousness.

What Morag demonstrates here is the ability to take the initiative and to implement alternative strategies. She is not prepared to take things lying down and to my mind this makes her a militant person. This view is substantiated when Morag talks about the relationships she has had, when she describes how she has moved from one relationship to another after coming to the conclusion that her partner of the time was not up to scratch; in other words, that he did not fit in with her needs, likes, dislikes and aspirations. For example, her first partner used to metaphorically pat her on the head, did not rate her highly in her work as an accountant and, furthermore, wanted children when she did not: 'Then I felt I'd got the wrong person, that we weren't really compatible'. As soon as she had reached this conclusion, she left. She had had great hopes for the second relationship with Carl, even thinking in terms of marriage and children. Carl was sociable, they had their work in common, there was always something going on at weekends and Carl 'would put as many ideas into the relationship as I would'. Then she found out that Carl was having an affair 'and I was let down'; and, furthermore, she reached the conclusion that he was never going to marry her. She therefore eventually entered a new relationship, with James, and left Carl.

This sequence shows her as testing the outside world and others for the extent to which they fit her requirements. Instead of questioning the latter and finding ways of mutually adjusting, she continues on her quest for the right world and the right partner. She had the feeling 'that it was James I could depend on, and that he would never leave me'. James has his good points, but there are many things about him with which she appears deeply dissatisfied, especially that he never wants to talk about her work and that she cannot talk business with him. Moreover, when talking about her first partner, she draws analogies with James: 'In fact he's more or less the same as James: worked very hard at work, but he didn't want to do anything at weekends'. It seems that Morag's strategy is always the same: she withdraws and takes unilateral action. This is the way she says she has learnt to cope with it. 'I actually walk away and say I'm going to sleep downstairs or whatever. I have learned to walk away'. Later, she explains this: 'If I think about a problem, I try and think about a course of action. Once I've decided on that course of action I follow it through'.

As her therapist, I will encourage Morag to explore the notion of assertiveness and independence being only one side of the coin – the other side involving other considerations and courses of action such as compromise, interdependency and adaptability. This does not mean that Morag has to be what she is not, as she seems to believe. 'The problem is that one would like to be able to change oneself to suit someone else', although she knows this won't work. 'But at the end of the day you can't do that. I think I've done that through different relationships. I've tried to be somebody that I'm not'. So Morag is aware that something has to be done, but comes down on the side of what is probably the wrong premise – that one should try to become what one is not – and, when that proves impossible, reaches an even more drastic conclusion: 'And so I have a feeling that they've either got to accept you as you are, or they've not, and they've got to make that decision. And they've not got to try and criticize the whole time'. These are all very extreme postures. It seems as though she is only considering things as being black or white, whereas she could come to appreciate that there is something in between – a whole area involving exploration, examination and discussion with others where compromise and adaptation from both sides may be possible and lead to more desirable outcomes.

My understanding of Morag is of someone who is very dissatisfied, angry and frustrated in her relationship with James, towards his ex-wife Paula and towards his children. Paula, who is 'hopeless', left James and the two children; and it was Morag who had to look after them for two years. Yet Paula still has some sort of hold over James: she 'sort of snapped her fingers and he shot straight round there'. What Morag cannot bear is being compared to Paula. I feel that the conflict within herself revolves around the fact that Paula, who has done all these terrible things and acted so irresponsibly, nevertheless is very manipulative and gets James to respond to her seeming helplessness, a quality that Morag despises: 'She does the helpless female bit which for various reasons exasperates me'. This is diametrically opposed to what Morag believes women should be like in society. In contrast, Morag is a very practical person, someone who just gets on with things, someone who possesses qualities towards which James was attracted, because 'I was fairly independent and didn't need looking after'. Yet now it is Morag who is being criticized by James. What also needs noting is the tone of envy. When Paula snaps her fingers and James goes running to her, then she is the woman of action and influence that Morag craves to be!

My understanding of this is that it is not just a matter of comparison with Paula, but more a matter of how Morag conceives of herself both in her work and at home. One of her aspirations is to be regarded and acknowledged as an efficient, independent, professional person who is standing up and fighting for women's rights and progress in a man's world. My suspicion is that, when she tries to create herself in this way, she is not paying attention to the needy person she really is as well, and this is something I will explore with her in order to try to identify her needs more clearly and to see how she can become more effective in getting her needs met. Perhaps this is what she is hinting at when she says: 'He frequently says that he would like to be looked after, and that I don't really take enough care of him. I suppose I feel it's a two-way thing'. This is very revealing in other ways: her life is completely predicated on action and independence, leaving little room for softer, quieter, vulnerable sides to both herself and James. They both yearn to be able to relax with each other, but hold the ambience taut out of fear. What this fear is needs to be explored.

James's children come separately on alternate weekends and James wants her to be there because 'he likes me being there, being the mother-hen'. Morag resents this. They invade her weekends; moreover, they are unhelpful and selfish, and 'so you suddenly feel crowded'. Morag realizes that, because there is no biological link between her and James's children, she is not as understanding, or willing to make 'all the excuses for them that you would with your own child'. She also acknowledges that 'they can sense I'm aggressive when they walk in'. What Morag is perhaps not seeing is that when she projects the children into the role of aliens invading her haven from the outside, with herself in the role of the victim who is being used and exploited, then the result will be missed chances and opportunities. The role of mother-hen, rather than being that of helpless victim, could be seen to be the role of power and influence in the family. I will explore with her the possibility of the children being in need of her, of their needing reassurance; and even more importantly the need for her not to feel threatened by them. Perhaps Morag needs to explore this whole situation from a different perspective. This links with her not having acknowledged the commitment she has taken on with these children; she has not really accepted James because of this. She wants him on her terms – without the children.

Morag comes across as someone who is interested in knowing and understanding herself better – how she thinks, how and why she acts in certain ways and, indeed, not only in her views and experience of life in general and her relationships in particular, but also in the meanings they have for her. She appears to be uncertain as to how to go about gaining these understandings. In her discourse with the therapist, Morag demonstrates a constant shift in direction, often breaking off in mid-sentence, sometimes going off on some slightly different tack; and therefore perhaps not sticking with something long enough to deliberate and ponder it long and deeply enough in order to be able to discern the meaning it has for her. A typical example is when she is talking about her relationship with Carl: 'But I suppose occasionally I look back with regret at that, because he . . . we had many things in common in a sense, but on the other hand he wasn't . . . you know, I could see that it would also be a problem to me'; that is, she does not allow herself to experience the regret, but immediately counteracts it. Thus she cannot learn from the past.

Morag often refers to herself in the third person, almost as though she is talking about someone else, as illustrated by her comments about herself and Carl: 'The feelings you had for him . . . so that it would let you go on and do something else'; or when she is talking about herself and James: "The problem is that one would like to be able to change oneself to suit someone else'. What is it that impels her to do this? She obviously takes her experience as an example of a general role. Could it be that she somehow distances herself from issues that are perhaps too difficult or painful to deal with? I will engage with her in an exploration of these areas. Something else which becomes apparent is that sometimes, just as Morag seems to be about to reflect on and perhaps comment on herself, she alters the focus on to someone else, becomes quite judgemental of them, and seems to apportion them with some blame: 'I feel that . . . I'm probably selfish . . . but I feel she's a very selfish person. She doesn't do anything if it doesn't suit her to do it'. I will try to make Morag aware of how she operates in this way and to examine it more closely. Morag sometimes seems more preoccupied with her own needs and desires rather than with self-awareness, or understanding of her interaction with others – let alone understanding of other people's needs and motivations!

Therapeutic possibilities

Morag appears to be the sort of client (as described by van Deurzen-Smith 1990) with whom one could work with from an existential approach. She is aware that her problems are about living, rather than a form of pathology; she seems ready to take part in an intense and very personal philosophical investigation. The very fact that she has agreed to take part in the present project is certainly indicative of this. She has a critical mind and demonstrates constantly that she is prepared to think for herself. The existential approach is particularly suitable for clients who are in search of meaning in their lives and who seek to clarify their personal ideology. It is also relevant for those who are in crisis. There are indications that Morag is such a client, as exemplified by some of the statements she makes about herself and her life: 'I'd like to understand why I enjoy doing things. I enjoy challenges'. 'But it's a question of how you can perhaps come to . . . either come to terms with it and work it. I suppose for me it's that I have to see a way forward'.

Morag is in a dilemma that expresses the conflicts of existence: how to be, what to be and who to be. An example of this is when she ponders: 'Is it right that I should always be wanting something new to go at, some new challenge? Should I just be accepting the way I am?' She is in a crisis situation regarding her relationship with James: 'The frightening feeling is, should I try to calm down, should I try not to do quite so much, for I suppose the happiness of the relationship?' This is leading her to examine it from the standpoint of a previous relationship with Carl. This may be bringing out un-resolved elements of that previous relationship which now threaten the current one. Morag is certainly experiencing conflicting thoughts and emotions which need looking at. She expresses very positive feelings about James: 'But on the whole he's there, he's there for me'; 'He is, you know, he is a very loving person'. She nevertheless also compares and contrasts this relationship to the previous one with Carl and it is important to clarify which elements of her past relationship are threatening to swamp, or at least deeply influence, her experience of her relationship with James. From her response to some of the further questions I put, I think it would be possible to work with her on exploring and clarifying the meaning and depth of the relationship she has, not only with James, but with Jessica, the other children and with herself.

From an existential approach standpoint, a primary view of suc-cess would be with regard to working with the client. I feel that Morag and I could engage in honest and challenging encounters with one another. The existential approach is more process-oriented rather than outcome-oriented and, as such, presents a number of arguments which would question the wisdom of approaching therapy from an outcome-success viewpoint (van Deurzen-Smith 1988; Spinelli 1989).

Generally, Morag appears open and willing and capable of serious reflection. There are indications that a deeper and more honest form of reflection can take place. However, there are one or two possible contraindications as well. I am not sure about the extent to which Morag may be too set in her perspective with regard to her self-concept for her to be willing to challenge or be challenged on a number of relational issues and conflicts that appear to spring from the self-concept she holds. An example of this that springs to mind is her view of herself as an independent, professional woman, who is not accorded the recognition, acknowledgement and respect that such a position deserves in her eyes; and how she applies this view in her relationships outside of the work situation. It seems as though she wants to hold the same position, and thus finds it difficult to hear and to consider seriously James's point of view. There is no hint of compromise or adjustment and indeed the very notion of compromise seems taboo, as it might be a threat to her sense of self. Her sense of self seems rather inflexible – asserting herself, demanding adjustments to her: 'He wants me to change roles, if you like, to be the nurturing mother-hen at the weekend, which doesn't lie easily on me'. There is no sense of inner openness here. If this is so, then it might make it difficult for us to engage with one another in such a way that my challenges will be heard and considered by her. If this were the case, then I would have to begin work with her on inner confidence, helping her to open up, and to work with her inner need.

Another possible difficulty is indicated in Morag's responses to some of my further questions, where she is very selective in what she responds to as well as the way in which she responds. For example, in response to my question about herself with regard to Paula and her (Paula's) influence on Morag and her relationship with James, Morag focuses away from herself and on to Paula's shortcomings: the unattractive aspects of her personality and her manipulative way of going about things. There are other examples of this inclination in Morag when confronted with something that challenges her to look quite closely at herself. This makes me think that there might be some difficulties in encouraging Morag to confront her own responsibilities in some of these matters and perhaps to look more closely at her own limitations, especially as they appear to match, complement and overlap with other people's.

The course of therapy

Existential therapy takes the form of a dialogue between therapist and client, rather than a questioning and answering procedure. Questions are therefore asked as little as possible. The approach is that of therapist and client working together in order to understand the inner and outer world of the client. It offers the client the means to examine, confront, clarify and reassess her understanding of life, the problems she has encountered, and the limits imposed upon the possibilities inherent in being-in-the-world. The interrelationship of therapist and client is an important aspect of the therapeutic encounter. This implies the approach is more concerned with qualitative factors that the therapist brings to the dialogue, than it is with the emphasizing of set skills and techniques. The therapist has to be there with an open mind and to be ready and willing to be flexible and to shift his stance when necessary. In order to do this, it is important to strive to put aside all preconceptions, beliefs, attitudes and prejudices in his work with the client. The therapist has constantly to bear in mind that the fundamental concern is with what matters most to the client, and should therefore avoid normative theories. At the same time, the client's own norms and values and direction will be explored and questioned against the wider perspective of basic principles of human living. As van Deurzen-Smith (1990) says: 'The attitude is non-directive, but is not directionless'.

The principal task is that of attempting entry into the client's experiential world in order that it may be exposed, examined, explored and (when necessary) challenged. The therapist is not passive in the encounter, but works actively to facilitate self-exploration, self-reflection, self-examination and greater self-understanding on the part of the client. The therapist probes, asks for clarification, asks the client to describe more fully and generally pursues enquiry in the spirit of exploration, so that if any questions are posed, they are along the following lines: 'What do you understand by this?', 'What does this mean to you?', or 'What is there about this that makes it so important to you?' Unlike therapists working from other therapeutic orientations, the existential therapist does not regard the client as suffering from some pathological condition and therefore does not have a notion of a 'cure'. By the same precept, he resists the temptation to change the client. Rather than trying to change her to fit into a preconceived idea of what he thinks she ought to be like, or the sort of life she should be living, the therapist will provide the environment, the space, the time and the understanding for the client to take stock of her life and her way of being in the world. Once she has gained a fuller and clearer understanding, what she wants to do with this is up to her: it is her decision. What the therapist can do is to point out aspects of a problem that the client may have overlooked, or make her aware of any lack of perspective or possibly her unwillingness to confront any issues that may arise. These could be presented as concrete evidence of aspects of the client's attitude to life. In like manner, aspects of the actual encounter between client and therapist could be reflected on and discussed in terms of evidence of the client's usual ways of relating.

In the course of the initial interview, there is an example of the last point I have made above. After a short silence, the therapist asked Morag what she was thinking. She replied: 'It flashed through my mind that I was supposed to keep talking, and what should I talk about, and should I go on to something different?' I would like to explore with her what she thinks the therapeutic process is about. She seems to have some ideas about there being some prescriptive pattern or way of behaving in therapy, and about what she is supposed to be doing in the session. Is there some connection with the way she relates in life generally? The verbatim report shows that she sometimes talks in terms of 'should's', 'shouldn't's' and 'must have's'; for example, when talking about her relationship with James's children. It would be worth exploring whether she has beliefs about what is expected of her in certain aspects of her life and how this affects the way she thinks and acts. The response to my additional question indicates that there is scope for this exploration.

There are a few assumptions Morag makes about life in general, and about people with whom she has relationships in particular, that might be worth examining with her. One of the assumptions she seems to be making is that James will never talk about her work. Her solution is therefore to ring Carl from time to time and discuss work matters with him instead. It appears that she convinces herself that she is right in her assumption and in her response to it. However, there is a hint of a niggling doubt: 'Maybe I'm being perhaps unfair to James in the . . . at the back of my mind comparing it to when I used to live with Carl'. Is the assumption correct? Or is it possible to examine the whole situation from other premises and perspectives? Another assumption she seems to have is that, because she has had to be militant in the professional sphere of her life in order to succeed as a woman 'in a man's world', that this may be a good way of dealing with relationships as well. There are examples of her taking unilateral action, which has far-reaching and long-lasting effects, often without involving the other party in discussion. This has not worked very well, and I would like to explore with her the possibility and feasibility of adopting different perspectives, attitudes and strategies, and considering some adjustment in her assumptions.

There are many instances of broken sentences, of Morag shifting direction half-way through sentences, and of some rephrasing in mid-sentence. I would want to make Morag aware of this as it happens and encourage her to slow down and to be more contemplative, not only about the content of what she is involved in presenting, but also about the way in which that process is occurring. One of the objectives, therefore, is to encourage Morag to slow down and take time *to be*, rather than *to act*.

These are examples of the way I will work with Morag: looking in detail, probing, examining and exploring, sometimes challenging and sometimes pointing out paradoxes, contrasts and discrepancies in what she presents. This process will occur in terms of the meanings

Morag attaches to various things; the need to be aware of and face up to certain limitations of the human condition as they perhaps apply to her; and the desirability of thinking through the consequences of choices, both past and future, and of the opinions, beliefs and values she holds dear.

All investigations and explorations conducted in the sessions will be geared towards the client gaining a greater understanding of what makes the world meaningful to her, as well as of an understanding of how she operates in the world in terms of power, control, influence and responsibility. The sessions will include challenges designed to get her to look anew at what she takes for granted and to help her to gain different perspectives on things.

The contract that I would offer Morag will be an open-ended one, with provision for a review of the therapy at any time, leading to continuation or termination. Morag appears to be a client with whom I could work in either the short term or over a longer period. My consideration would be to offer her a contract that allows her to reflect sufficiently upon herself, to free herself up to facing the future in a fuller way than before, but at the same time not making her dependent upon the therapy or the therapist. At the same time, I would guard against fitting in with Morag's action-packed efficiency. Therapy may be the place for her to learn to breathe and expand, taking the time to discover unrecognized yearnings and needs, instead of doing the efficient goal-oriented fixing job she may be expecting.

Problem areas

In the existential approach, the engagement of therapist and client in working together in an exploration and clarification of the various relational orientations of the client's existence is regarded as a central enterprise. This requires me, as therapist, to suspend or bracket my own bias and assumptions, so that I am better able to hear and attend to the client. This is not easily accomplished. The implication is that I, as therapist, have already got assumptions about the outcomes of therapy with Morag, as well as the difficulties in getting there. If problems appear, I think they will be about how our relationship develops. In other words, it is the kind of encounter we have which might bring difficulties. The sort of problems I might have may be to do with listening and hearing; in letting Morag live her own life; and in phrasing comments and questions in ways that are not seen as judgements or new rules for her to try to live by.

Another question is that of the relationship. Although it thrives on both contact and tension, problems and dangers arise either when it is one where all that is experienced is a friendly ear or, alternatively, when the tension it provokes become destructive. The main problems therefore would be with regard to the kind of relationship that Morag and I construct, the clarity of its boundaries and possibilities, and the willingness on both our parts to challenge the underlying assumptions that we bring to it about ourselves, the other, and each other.

This therapy relies on a certain attitude and commitment on the part of both client and therapist. The problem for me as therapist will be to reach sufficient depth of clarity and openness to be able to venture along with Morag into difficult areas, and to explore with her how her experience fits into the wider map of her existence. I will be involved in this exploration and will therefore also be changed in the process. The problem is whether I will be open and willing enough to enable this to happen. The commitment from the client's side is a willingness to look at her assumptions, values and aspirations with a view to taking a new direction. There is some evidence to show that this may be something of a problem when working with Morag. She sometimes hesitates, changes direction in mid-sentence or does not complete what she started out to explore. This may be indicative of an avoidance in confronting certain issues. At other times, Morag seems to move away from self-examination, and therefore from self-awareness, by shifting the focus away from herself and on to others, often homing in on their faults and shortcomings. Sometimes she is quite judgemental and blaming of them.

The problems outlined above are by no means insurmountable, although much will depend upon the relationship developing into one where openness, trust and commitment to work with issues and difficulties become possible.

Criteria for successful outcome

The existential approach is much more process-oriented rather than outcome-oriented and, in this regard, success would not be measured against some preconceived, stipulated outcome goal. For example, it would not be a case of resolving issues so that Morag has a clear route, but rather getting her to confront the contradictory views she holds, putting them into perspective with the paradoxes of living. For example, Morag thinks she must focus on James's positive side – otherwise, the relationship may be threatened. It may be that in order to make it positive, Morag has to face the negative side as well. A task in therapy would be to help her face the fact that she is not aware of how paradox occurs in life. Another would be for Morag to try to find some means of acknowledging the contradictory views she holds and of living with them. It is not a question of one view being right and the other being wrong. They are two sides of the same coin. Both express aspects of Morag's being. Seen in that way, they both deserve to exist and to be acknowledged and addressed.

There is a recognition in the existential approach that many life issues do not have a single successful outcome possibility, but rather reveal the necessity for the client to face and come to terms with a number of dilemmas that cannot ever be fully resolved in an ideal fashion. In this sense of the term 'positive outcome', what is being described is the client's willingness and ability to confront and find an adequate means of living with the uncontrollable stimuli of life, rather than it being a question of problem-resolution. While there may or may not be any observable behavioural changes in Morag, this in itself need not necessarily suggest any negative outcome. The issue might more accurately be around Morag's experience of herself as a responsible person choosing these behaviours, rather than experiencing herself as a victim of them. I can envisage that some part of my working with Morag may very well be to assist her in coming to terms with some of life's contradictions, rather than trying to change them. In my experience, it is when a client faces up to reality in this way that they eventually find a satisfactory way forward.

As my approach is more concerned with process than outcome in the terms I have described, all the investigations conducted by Morag and myself will hopefully eventually lead to Morag gaining a greater understanding of what makes the world meaningful to her. The idea is to assist her in finding purpose and motivation in her life, as well as to facilitate the elimination of a number of misleading or irrelevant motivations, as they are encountered and exposed in our working together. Part of this work will be geared towards assisting Morag to become more self-aware and more ready and willing to engage in self-examination, and through this to gain a greater understanding of herself in the world. This aspect of the work may involve my challenging of her perspectives and assumptions and may often focus on her view of the world and her role in it: how she operates in the world, and on what basis she makes judgements and decisions. Rather than aiming at specified goals and outcomes, I would bear in mind that the existential approach embraces the notion that life is one long process of constant change and transformation. I will therefore enter and be involved in this process with Morag by assisting her to become more aware; for example, gaining insight into the possibility of reinterpreting a situation, and opting for more constructive positions, may lead to a change for the better. My earnest endeavours will be directed towards assisting Morag to gain more clarity concerning the options and choices that are available to her, and to gain an understanding of the bases on which she makes judgements and decisions.

I will also aim for Morag to achieve a greater awareness and sensitivity to the results of her decisions, judgements and subsequent actions on others, on her relationships and on herself. Part of the work will be focused upon considering the possibility of breaking old, destructive habits of both thought and action, as well as considering, for example, where priorities lie, thus enabling choices to be made with more understanding than previously. I will encourage Morag to look at how she deals with difficulties, such as issues or questions that arise, or situations that seem threatening. There are examples of how Morag deals with them by withdrawing and taking some unilateral action. I will encourage her to re-examine these occasions and situations and to consider whether those were the only options available to her.

Finally, Morag appears to be locked into some aspects of the past, which in turn seems to be having an adverse and even destructive effect on her present relationships, especially the one she has with James. I will work with Morag towards understanding that the past is flexible and open to interpretation. While the facts relating to the past, as they are recollected, cannot be easily altered, what can be altered are one's fixed views of the past. It is possible to reinterpret the same events and experiences in different ways. What I will try to get Morag to see is the influence on her future of her views and beliefs related to the past, and I will try to indicate to her how to a great extent she herself has control over this. There is every possibility that she can change this and open up new vistas for the future for herself.

Summary

Morag appears to be a client who is in a crisis situation, particularly with regard to her relationship with James. She is aware of this and wants to do something about it. Morag shows in her discourse with the therapist that she can be open and capable of serious and earnest reflection. It seems to me that she is the sort of client with whom one could work from an existential approach, as she consistently demonstrates an awareness of her problems being about living, rather than about some sort of pathology. She is searching for meaning in her life as well as seeking to clarify her personal ideology.

In the existential approach, therapist and client engage in a process of examining, exploring and clarifying issues, problems, feelings, beliefs, assumptions and situations in the client's life, which should lead to greater self-understanding on the part of the client. There are certainly a few assumptions Morag makes about life in general and about significant others in her life in particular which might bear examination in the way I have described. It seems as though Morag and I could work together in this way. The principal task for the therapist is to enter the experiential world of the client in order that it may be examined, explored and sometimes challenged. The inter-relationship of therapist and client is therefore an important aspect of the therapeutic encounter.

I am sure all the therapists concerned with this project are ex-tremely grateful to Morag for being willing to engage in this experi-ment. For my part, I hope that she may have found my particular approach, emphasis and slant to be both challenging and attentive to her experience.

Further reading

Deurzen-Smith, E. van (1988). *Existential Counselling in Practice*. London: Sage.

Deurzen-Smith, E. van (1990). Existential therapy. In W. Dryden (ed.), *Individual Therapy: A Handbook*. Buckingham: Open University Press.

May, R. (1983). *The Discovery of Being: Writings in Existential Psychology*. New York: W.W. Norton.

Spinelli, E. (1989). *The Interpreted World: An Introduction to Phenomenological Psychology*. London: Sage.

Yalom, I. (1980). *Existential Psychotherapy*. New York: Basic Books.

ANTHEA MILLAR

ADLERIAN THERAPY

The therapist

As a counsellor, I wondered how it would be writing a chapter in a book in a series entitled *In Search of a Therapist*. My choice to go ahead reflects the blurred boundaries I perceive between much counselling and psychotherapy practice.

My background as a counsellor begins with my work as a speech therapist. Working with people who had suffered major neurological trauma, I witnessed the ripple effect when one individual experiences change, and how this has repercussions for all those in his or her social sphere. This underlined for me the social connectedness and interdependence of humanity.

These two themes of social connectedness and communication have emerged frequently in my own therapy and it is not surprising that I felt drawn to Adler's Individual Psychology. This stresses the indivisible nature of the human personality, and emphasizes that we can only understand our behaviour within a social context. This choice occurred after I had completed a course in Current Theories in Psychotherapy, where I was introduced to the viewpoints of Jung, Klein, Winnicott, Berne and Adler. I am glad of this broad base prior to beginning my counsellor training, as these and other approaches continue to provide valuable additional building blocks to an Adlerian foundation stone.

My counselling training was highly practical. The trainers took what I found to be an exciting and radical approach in exposing us initially to family counselling, where we were directly supervised as we worked with families. The learning was immediate, the theory being introduced alongside or after the practice. Gaining an understanding first of the family and its dynamics set the scene for me to understand the individual in a holistic way. This training also reflects the Adlerian philosophy that insight alone is not enough. For growth there needs to be action, whether in thought, feeling or directly visible behaviour. This also links with the need to have awareness and connection with both our own inner state *and* the outer world. The development of *Gemeinschaftsgefühl* (community feeling) is a crucial factor of Adlerian psychology and psychotherapy.

I work full-time as a counsellor, trainer and supervisor, practising in very varied ways, and with both short- and long-term contracts. In common with many Adlerian practitioners, I aim to use processes that are adapted to fit the client, that may be common to other approaches, while remaining congruent with the basic concepts of Individual Psychology. So 'techniques' might include imaging, art work, role play and psychodrama, alongside Adlerian processes of understanding and reorienting the client's subjective reality through work with early recollections, use of paradox, challenge, encouragement and homework assignments.

I continue to value learning from other therapeutic approaches, and I see no conflict in incorporating aspects from seemingly diverse viewpoints into my work. My interest and commitment to developing skills and understanding in intercultural counselling and therapy is perhaps a reflection of this integrative approach.

Further information requested

Presenting the questions that follow in this formal way is not my normal practice, although I sometimes contract with a client to carry out a structured lifestyle assessment as outlined here. I will listen to Morag as she shares her story, and I will explore and develop tentative hypotheses informally as we build a working relationship. My questions emerge from the flow of the session, when the issues present themselves more naturally.

The current situation

1 *What do you hope for and want in coming to therapy?*
   I hope that I would be able to understand why I get a
   particular feeling of ... frustration or anger ... I hope that I
   will be able to ... rationalize them ... it's almost like
   something one's got to get over.

2 *You have talked a little about your work and your relationships with
   your partners. What about friendship and leisure time? How does this
   go in your life at present?*

'I was going to say what leisure time?' [Morag continues by saying that she does have a few times each week when she swims and sees her girlfriends, but James does not share her pleasure in socializing.] 'It's one of the things I feel sad about because I am quite a sociable person . . . It's one area of my life that I would like, I'd like more social contact'.

3 *How is your sexual life at present? How was it with previous partners?*
'I always get very attracted to people to start with, but when you've been with them a few years I find it more difficult to feel stimulated'. Morag says that she experiences this with James also. Carl was the only person she wanted to make love to more than he wanted.

4 *You've said that you've tried to be somebody you are not. Who are you? When do you feel most yourself?*
I feel most myself when I'm doing my own work, when I'm learning . . . when I'm experiencing something new . . . I know I have the capability of going in more or less any direction I like and making a success of it.

Lifestyle assessment

5 *Do you have brothers and/or sisters? If so, can you list them all, in descending order, beginning with the oldest, with the age differences between them and you. Include siblings who have died or miscarried.*

Brother	Sister	Morag	Sister
(3 years older)	(18 months older)		(18 months younger)

6 *Who was most different from you? How?*
My elder sister . . . well, she's the one that [*laughs*] I have the most arguments with . . . she wasn't as bright as I was. It may have been because she was dyslexic, but she always trailed in her class, whereas I was always the top of the class. She was much better looking than I was . . . she always had a string of boyfriends . . . She was probably more temperamental, whereas I was more logical.

7 *Who was most like you? How?*
Possibly my brother because he again was more logical . . . business-minded . . . can probably go for whatever he wanted to go for.

8 *What kind of child were you?*
An observant child really . . . I let my brother and sister,
mainly my sister fight all the battles . . . get the rules set . . . I
can remember as a child enjoying watching and listening to
adults and . . . taking a back seat when things were happening
to see how things were going to pan out, and then going for
the . . . er, the best way. I enjoyed school tremendously. I
enjoyed playing lots of sports . . . We just had our friends and
I think probably belonging to teams . . . I was team captain,
house captain, head girl . . . that was a bit of a strain that . . .
[*laughs*].

9 *Looking through the eyes of yourself as a young child, how would you
describe your brother and sisters?*
Brother to be respected . . . if one got in a fight he would
win, so I sussed out fairly early on that it was best to have
him on my side. My elder sister quite an interesting person
because she was such a rebel, but maybe not very bright . . . I
sussed that out fairly early on. My younger sister then was
sort of roly-poly and sort of a happy person . . . a little
bundle of fun really.

10 *Who fought and argued? Who played together? Who took care of
whom?*
It was usually my elder sister and my younger sister against
my brother and I if we fought . . . we all played together . . . I
can't remember any of us taking care of any of us.

11 *Who, if at all, had a handicap or prolonged illness?*
Morag's elder sister had difficulty reading and was prone to accidents.

12 *Looking through the eyes of yourself as a young child, how would you
describe (a) your mother and (b) your father?*
[Mother]: A mixture of loving and cuddly. If you were
upset . . . she would be there . . . But busy, apart from that it
would be: 'Go away and play' . . . You know she had a lot to
do . . . but she'd always be playing things like snap . . . if she
could spare the time.
[Father]: Distant. Unemotional. I don't think I ever did
know what he was thinking, ever. Unless one of us was ill,
and then he was quite good at soothing the brow with a
cool hand . . . He never did much with us really.

13 *What kind of relationship existed between your mother and father?*
My first reaction was to say don't know. Um . . . they argued
. . . it appears to me that they either were . . . kind of getting
on with their own things, or they were arguing . . . my father
. . . was not really very good, he had affairs . . . wasn't very
good at providing money . . . was absent a lot of the time,
and I think all these things hurt my mother quite a lot.

14 *What relationship did they have with each of you as children?*
Morag felt her elder sister 'could wind her father round her little
finger'. She has no memory of him being interested or affectionate
towards herself. She experienced her mother treating her brother in
a special way when he went to boarding school, which 'even now
infuriates me a bit . . . my younger sister I don't remember anybody
doing anything particular with . . . my mother and my older sister
used to fight . . .'.

15 *If there were other key figures, describe any influences you feel they
had in your life.*
There were au pairs that she felt attached to, and various people that
stayed that were interesting, but none was a key influence: 'it was
really part of my people-watching state'. She then talked of her
father's influence in his value of 'stickability'.

16 *How would you describe the atmosphere in your home?*
There was always lots going on and we laughed a lot. One
memory of us being round the table . . . everybody
laughing . . . hurly-burly sort of thing.

17 *What were the most important family values? Can you think of a
motto, spoken or unspoken, that expresses the values present at home?*
My father was very keen . . . on getting everything exactly
right . . . 'stickability' . . . if you've decided to go for
something, you went for it, and didn't give up . . . you strive
to win. My mother would encourage everybody to be as
independent as they could . . . and do whatever was just
outside their grasp. [After the session, Morag wrote]: One
other family trait that could well have had more of an effect
on me than I realized: We had a rota of jobs to be done
before we could go out to play. [Mottoes]: In freedom I will
be peaceful; People are individuals, and they are allowed to
be individuals; Life is not fair [from mother].

Early recollections

18 *Think back as far as you can remember, to something that happened
when you were very young, ideally before you were 7 years old. It can
be anything at all, good or bad, important or unimportant, but it does
need to be a specific incident, something that happened only once. How
old were you? Which part of the memory stands out most clearly? That
is, if you could take a snapshot of the most significant part of the
memory, what would it show? What was (is) your feeling related
to that snapshot? Share a further two to four memories in the same
way, identifying the 'snapshot', and the feeling associated with the
snapshot.*

With the first memory, Morag was asked for all these aspects. The
later recollections came in one continuous flow, and a specific request for the age, the snapshot and feeling was not given by the
therapist. Given the opportunity to work directly with Morag, I
would have focused her down further to gain the 'snapshot' and
associated feeling.

Early recollection 1: age 3 or 4 years

It was my birthday, and we lived in a bungalow. The front
was quite close to the road . . . we were all dressed up in
party dresses, and we had a sofa that was right next to the
window, and I can remember several of us children getting
on the sofa, and I think some sailors or something like that
were going by on the pavement outside, and I was standing
up at the window shouting, 'Come and join the party!' What
my mother would have . . . [*laughs*] if they actually had, I
don't know.
[Snapshot]: Us in party dresses on the sofa . . . shouting out
of the window.
[Feeling]: I don't know why I've remembered it . . . I don't
know if we got told off for shouting . . . I guess I knew, we
thought we were being a bit naughty, because you shouldn't
shout out of the window anyway, and er . . . I don't know,
I'm puzzled by it.

Early recollection 2

When we moved from that bungalow to a house, my mother
had sent all of us children away to, um, to be at somebody
else's house while they moved, and I can remember us being
given sort of mathematical games to play, you know on a
sheet, and I didn't want to know. All I wanted to do was to

be back with my mother. I was very homesick and I think I made everybody's life miserable until I did get – I was allowed home before the others. And um . . . that's one thing that sticks out.

Early recollections 3 and 4

The next two memories given were regular happenings rather than a specific event. Morag relates how they used to dress up as Ali Baba in her grandmother's bloomers and skirt, and she was sure that her grandmother would have 'had an absolute fit if she knew what was happening to her bloomers'. Also, they used to go for long walks in the country with 'the whole gang . . . probably an au pair or whatever'.

Early recollection 5

Fell downstairs . . . the house we moved to was actually a maisonette. It had some . . . metal stairs that went up to this enormous big terrace, and the house, which was sort of Georgian, was at the back, and, er, I was carrying a very heavy suitcase down . . . I think there was probably something like dressing-up clothes in the suitcase, and I was hanging on with one hand, and carrying this. And I must have let go with this hand because I actually tumbled and fainted. [Snapshot and feeling]: Landing up at the bottom of these metal stairs, being very embarrassed because I'd fainted, I actually, er, peed. Whatever I had on was a little damp. And sitting there, and obviously my mother being concerned that I'd got concussion, or something like that.

Early recollection 6: age 7 years

I can remember when I went to Brownies, so I must have been pretty young there. We went, I . . . my, my sister was older, with me, and we went to Brownies. And then there was this footpath that you had to go down to come away from the hut. And there was a high fence and there were some apples, um . . . and we got on the wall and picked some of the apples on the way home. And my sister snitched [laughs].
[Snapshot and feeling]: I can remember my mother really telling us off, and saying we could go to prison and jail . . . and being really frightened, that this would, you know, this calamity would befall us.

Dreams

19 *Did you have any recurrent dreams as a child? Do you have any recurrent dreams now? If so, what stands out to you most vividly in the dream? What feeling is associated with this? How do you feel when you wake up?*

Morag had no memory of a childhood recurrent dream, but related the following recent recurrent dream:

> The only recurrent one that I have is this feeling that my daughter – got lots of balconies in my house – that my daughter is, has climbed on to the balcony and is falling off. I mean that tends to wake me up a few times. Probably more when she was little. I haven't had it for a while now. It's just, you know, a little heart-stopping.
> [Feeling]: It's certainly really frightening.
> [Feeling on waking]: Relieved that it was a dream.

Assessment

From the first minute of the session, I begin making tentative hypotheses about Morag's movement through life. I am wondering if her late arrival and what is described as this 'inevitable lack of time and space for herself' is to be an important theme in therapy.

From the written word, I assume that Morag is white and British, but regret not checking this out as I want to be aware of her race and culture. I discover she is a professional woman, about my age, and find myself connecting with her, particularly with the 'time and space' issue. I make a mental note that I need to watch this identification; it may blur my hearing Morag clearly.

As Morag tells her story through the written word, I really miss the dimension of non-verbal communication. However, from her calm description of her aggression, I guess she wants to avoid exposure of painful feelings. As I read on further, I structure the detail of the here-and-now issues in three main areas (life tasks): How does she experience work, both in the home and outside it? How does she see her social life? How does she experience intimate relationships? I also look for recurring themes and patterns and so begin to get a sense of her Lifestyle (the Adlerian term for her life movement).

Work

This area seems a central pivot for Morag, touching all other parts of her life. She initially presents herself through her two successful work roles. I notice her pride in these achievements, and experience an energy as she describes her pleasure in facing challenge. This is underlined in her response to my question, 'When do you feel most yourself?': 'When I'm doing my own work, when I'm learning. I feel me when I see the success of the business'. This would seem to begin to address her wanting 'to understand why I enjoy challenges'. At this point, I wonder if a key aspect of Morag's private logic is something like: to exist and be me I *must* keep moving and striving onwards towards further success. This theme seems to come up again when she talks of her role as a woman in the world of work: 'I don't feel I've got on as far as I could have done had I been a man because I had to work twice as hard as everybody else to get where I got'.

Morag takes a different tone around the work at home, resenting expectations to play 'mother-hen': 'I get quite cross (with James) that he keeps trying to push me into the traditional role'. Yet there seems also a sense of obligation to be a good step-parent, parent and homemaker. Linked with this I have a feeling of the competition between her and James's ex-wife who is 'just so hopeless'. I wonder if this echoes the relationship Morag experienced with her elder sister (see 'Lifestyle assessment').

Friendships and leisure time

There is a major discrepancy between her and James in their views around socializing: 'James is not a very sociable person . . . and it's one of the things I feel sad about because I am quite a sociable person'. This theme of enjoying socializing comes out in her early memories, and is further emphasized in strong family values: 'If anybody came to the door you always made them feel very welcome'. With this deeply embedded value Morag seems in conflict between how she 'ought' to be with her stepchildren (i.e. welcoming them and compromising her own needs), and the aggression she actually feels. The theme of her needing to keep on the move also comes up in describing leisure activities: 'I've always been on the move'; 'To relax . . . I have to be doing something else . . . something totally different'.

Intimacy

I had difficulty in getting down to writing this section, finding myself flitting back continuously to the other areas of Morag's life. I feel now that this 'stuckness' may echo Morag's difficulty in facing painful thoughts and feelings around intimacy. Her pattern of emotional and sexual intimacy seems to follow the recurring theme of enjoying the newness and challenge initially, but 'when things don't go well, you start thinking the grass is greener elsewhere'. Now it seems this belief is being challenged in her present relationship with James: 'I'm fairly determined that I want this relationship to stay'. Her private logic of 'Look forward rather than back' is also confronted when she acknowledges the unresolved grief around the ending of her relationship with her previous partner Carl.

In talking about intimacy, Morag touches on the fundamental pull between wanting to please others, and to be herself: 'The problem is that one would like to be able to change oneself to suit someone else. But at the end of the day you can't . . . I've tried to be somebody that I'm not . . .'.

Lifestyle assessment

My aim now is to see how these concerns fit into Morag's overall characteristic pattern of movement. Here I use the process of lifestyle assessment from which I can do some fine-tuning of my first hunches. I want to understand how she created a meaning for herself in her first world – the family, which acts as a 'life map' for her perception of the world now. Psychologically a second and middle child between two sisters, with an older brother, she watches the world acutely, learning 'the best way' by 'taking a back seat when things were happening to see how things were going to pan out'. Her older sister, 'the rebel, but not very bright', would seem to be the key player or *Gegenspieler*. Morag found her place by taking the opposite path – being the bright, responsible, cooperative one; also the one that strives harder. She does not perceive herself having a special relationship with either of her parents, unlike her brother and older sister, 'which even now infuriates me'.

Her perception of intimacy can perhaps be seen in the way she describes her parents' relationship: 'they were either getting on with their own thing . . . or they were arguing'. (An echo of her relationship with James perhaps?) This contrasts with her positive description of the family atmosphere: 'always lots going on and we laughed a lot'. It seems when Morag is in the midst of happy action she feels a clear sense of place, although she also wants (but does not expect) one-to-one specialness.

The early recollections (ERs) provide valuable projective data of Morag's view of life, a metaphor of her private logic. What follows are my initial hypotheses, which I will share with Morag for her verification and probable modification during therapy. These guesses are in the form of 'I am . . . People are . . . Life is . . . Therefore I . . .' statements:

- ER 1: I am a close observer of an interesting world which can pass me by. People should come and join in *my* fun. Therefore, I must dress up (put on a front) and (only) then can I shout out to be heard.
- ER 2: The world takes me away from those I love. I can only get what I want in relationships by making everybody's life miserable. Therefore, I have to change myself to suit others in order to avoid hurt and guilt.
- ER 5: The world is full of enormous hurdles and burdens. If I let go, I lose control and fall into embarrassing situations. Therefore, I must hang on, keeping up appearances.
- ER 6: I feel really frightened of a calamity befalling me if people find me out. Therefore, I must avoid exposure.
- Recurrent dream: Adler understood recurrent dreams as a repeated answer to a repeated problem. I see this as very similar to ER 5: Morag's fear of falling, or losing prestige, in the face of a world full of hurdles.

A recurring theme is that of Morag needing to keep up a front, to maintain control of feelings, and to avoid being 'found out'. My guess is that her presenting concern of aggressive feelings towards the stepchildren underlines her conflict in not being the 'nice' person she feels she should be, which is also around in her relationship with James. The other issue she presented initially was around 'why I enjoy challenges'. Here I sense that her continual urge to strive harder was a pattern she created within her family as a way to belong and have meaning.

Awareness of Morag's many resources and assets and her level of social interest and contribution is also an important aspect of assessment. Morag's striving onwards also resources her to meet new challenges and take risks. This is frequently in the form of initiating opportunities from which others can benefit, such as her mobile catering business. She enjoys cooperating in a team, and has leadership skills. Along with this, she is also independent and self-sufficient.

Finally, I go back to reflect on my first hunch about the 'time and space for herself' issue. This does seem to be a central theme for Morag, a pull between freedom and responsibility, a fundamental existential issue that is perhaps at the heart of all therapy.

Therapeutic possibilities

On first reading the transcript, it felt right to be working with Morag. With further reflection, I continue to feel that we can work together usefully. What indications are there that therapy can work well?

Morag is clear in presenting her wants in therapy. She wishes to understand and deal with her aggressive feelings towards her step-children, and to explore why she always wants to be on the move. Although other underlying issues emerge, we have a base for a mutual alignment of therapy goals. From this we have the beginnings of establishing a cooperative working relationship.

Morag's life in the here-and-now has a good number of supportive elements, and she strives for significance on the useful side of life. She is well established and respected in her work, and has a solid core of friends. I feel that with this backup from work and friend-ships, she will be in a stronger position to explore and challenge her private logic, specifically in the area of intimate relationships and the conflicts about her sense of self.

I see Morag's enjoyment of challenge and risk as being positive in terms of therapy success but also as a possible barrier, which I will explore later in the section entitled 'Problem areas'. My use of the Adlerian approach will include challenging Morag's mistaken beliefs and thinking. As she presents her 'intellectualizing' rather than 'feel-ing' self to the world, a cognitive and educative approach will, I think, be an acceptable 'way in' for Morag to begin reassessing her view of life. The Adlerian approach allows for a wide range of strat-egies and processes that are fitted to the needs of each client. This encourages me, as Morag's therapist, to be flexible and creative, which I see as contributing to a constructive outcome.

Assessing contraindications of success in therapy with Morag, I will go through a mental checklist of issues, which will need ongoing review. Does Morag want therapy or was she coerced to come? Is Morag's mental state such that she can respond to a formal regular therapy contract? Are there any blurred boundary issues regarding our relationship outside therapy? Are there major diversities between our value systems, and cultural or racial identity that could be detri-mental to building a successful working relationship? Do the issues presented go beyond my professional competence and experience?

While not complacent that my work with Morag will be plain sailing, I do not at present see problems with any of the issues raised above. I feel hopeful that in working in a collaborative way with Morag, reviewing and maintaining focus on mutually decided aims, we can work together towards a positive outcome.

The course of therapy

Following an Adlerian framework for Morag's therapy, I will have in mind four key goals that link with four therapeutic phases. Each of these phases is interwoven with the others, creating a fluid rather than linear structure. They involve:

- establishing and maintaining a working therapeutic relationship with Morag;
- exploring and gaining insight into Morag's psychological dynamics;
- facilitating Morag's development of self-understanding;
- encouraging Morag to make new choices (reorientation).

When Morag first enters the therapy room, I invite her to sit wherever she feels comfortable from a choice of chairs of equal height, seating myself opposite her in one of the remaining chairs. I go over the initial contract, including my fee, and clarification that this first one-hour session is a preliminary assessment, from which we can make a joint decision on the best way to proceed. I explain the confidentiality code, and tell her I keep notes that she has access to if she wishes. I also ask her permission to tape-record the sessions which I will be taking to supervision, and erasing immediately afterwards.

In this first session, I listen to Morag's story, paraphrasing, reflecting, and providing empathy. Adler felt it essential to develop an empathic understanding of the client's subjective perception of the world, and to communicate this to her. If I can enable Morag to feel deeply understood and accepted, she is more likely to focus on what she wants from therapy and so establish goals. Morag already has some clear idea of her wants in therapy, which she clarified further in response to my question, 'What do you hope for and want in coming to therapy?' (see 'Further information requested'). I may also add at this point 'What have you done about this until now?', and 'How would your life be different if you did not have these concerns?'

From this first moment of meeting Morag, I begin to gather information, attending closely to her non-verbal and verbal communication to gain insight into her psychological mode of operating through life. The information gathering at this stage is carried out informally as we build a relationship and I listen to the presenting problems. Near the end of this first session, having clarified her immediate therapy goals, I ask her what she wants to do regarding future therapy with me. I feel positive about seeing Morag if she so chooses.

On her deciding to continue, I will suggest that we meet for a run of six weekly sessions, and then review the therapy process and her goals for it. At this early stage in my knowledge of Morag, I sense that it may be most helpful for her to have a time-limited contract of perhaps a further ten to fifteen sessions after this review, with a clearly marked ending point. I feel this could be important in terms of unclear endings in previous relationships. Knowing the point of ending near the beginning can maintain a valuable focus for therapy.

During the first few sessions, I will continue to listen carefully to Morag's story in the here-and-now, while making an informal assessment of her lifestyle, paying close attention to her feelings, motives, beliefs and goals. As well as exploring feelings to develop empathy, I will go beyond this to explore the beliefs that underlie her feelings. One way I frequently use to assess this within the flow of therapy is to ask for early memories connected with the feelings. For example, as Morag talks of her angry feelings towards her step-children, and then says 'It's almost like something one's got to get over', I will ask her to stay with the angry feeling and thought, and recall any specific early childhood memory that comes into her mind at that point. As she recalls a specific memory, I will ask her what stands out most vividly, both in terms of the visual image and the feeling that goes with it. I will then ask for the thought that prompts this feeling.

Adler believed that we only recall memories that have meaning for us now, and are consistent with our current views of ourselves. As Morag shares her memories, I do not assess them as events that are causal to her way of being. I view them as a metaphor that helps me understand how she sees the world, what her life goals are, what motivates her, what she believes in and what she values. The choice of memory will also have a connection with how Morag perceives her present situation.

Information about her first family (family constellation) may emerge naturally. I will fill in any gaps with the kind of questions I asked in the more formal lifestyle assessment described earlier.

In the third phase of therapy, I aim to help Morag to understand and have insight into her private logic. This needs a tactful and respectful approach. You have read some of my guesses in the Assessment section. I will keep these in mind during the sessions, and when I feel the time is right I will put forward a tentative challenge. Here are some possible examples:

> Morag, when you talk of your anger, I notice you are quite calm. Could it be that to lose control feels embarrassing and frightening?

> You have been talking of wanting to understand why you enjoy challenges. I had a sense that you found your place in the family by striving on towards success. [Here I wait for Morag's verification.] I'm wondering if to stop pushing forward feels as if you might lose your place in the world?

It could be that my hypotheses are off the mark, but I do not have to be right. Morag is the expert on herself, and will be able to verify or modify my interpretations. Her understanding of her private logic is only just below consciousness and my role is to help it to be verbalized using tact and empathy. Private logic consists of over-generalizations, and unrealistic ideas; and once voiced, the logic will begin to lose its dominating strength. Alongside the challenge of mistaken perceptions, I will also be encouraging Morag to take note of her many assets. This process of encouragement is basic to all the phases, but has a particularly important role at this stage in giving Morag strength to see she has the power to choose and so act differently if she wishes.

As well as working on the immediate goals of her feelings of anger and issues of challenge, I sense it is likely that Morag will wish to look further at her unresolved grief with Carl, and also the central pull she experiences between responsibility and freedom. The insights from the lifestyle analysis will have equal relevance to these issues, as private logic refers to a total pattern of movement.

I see many ways of working with Morag during this third phase, and later at the reorientation phase. I will go with Morag's flow and, as appropriate, draw from a wide range of procedures, many from other approaches. For example, she may connect well initially to a more cognitive approach when beginning to work through her irrational fears and thoughts about her aggressive feelings. The use of Socratic questioning is a fundamental tool in Adlerian therapy, and will help Morag be a co-investigator into her self-defeating patterns. When we have built a more trusting relationship, I feel empty chair, imaging or art work may enable her to address her unresolved relationship issues, if she chooses to move towards these areas of exploration. Regarding the 'myself' or 'mother-hen' conflict, I may introduce a process from psychodrama, encouraging these two parts of her to enter into dialogue, and work towards integration. I will continue to work with Morag's early recollections as metaphors of her private logic that she can be helped to reframe, whether through spoken or written words, art, imaging or role play.

The fourth phase of reorientation is about supporting and resourcing Morag as she puts her insights into action. I will encourage Morag to catch herself repeating old patterns, focusing only on those that Morag wants to change. Adler pioneered the strategy of paradoxical intention, and this might be helpful if Morag feels stuck in a pattern she wants to change. Here I will join with her resistance rather than oppose it, and suggest she consciously exaggerates the debilitating thoughts and behaviours for a short period of time. This may enable Morag to begin to feel in control of the very behaviours she has felt enslaved by.

Task setting and homework assignments may be a valuable part of this phase. However, I sense from my knowledge of Morag, that once she has insight, she is likely to initiate putting this understanding into action with minimum input from me, apart from ongoing encouragement.

The timing of ending therapy with Morag will be discussed after we have reviewed progress. Earlier, I suggested a possibility of a further ten to fifteen sessions after review. If this time-span does seem appropriate, then I will plan to address our ending very specifically in the last two to three sessions. I will encourage Morag to review her experience of therapy, actively acknowledging her progress. It will also be valuable to explore her experience of this ending, as it may connect with old feelings of loss and grief. This can be an opportunity to create an ending that feels right for her, for which she is in control. It is unlikely that this ending will mark a neat resolution of all Morag's concerns. However, I am hopeful that Morag will feel resourced within herself to continue the process of growth and change.

Problem areas

I anticipate a number of problems in the course of therapy with Morag, although none feels too daunting at this point. Perhaps the first is my own identification with Morag. I also enjoy challenges, and can feel compelled to meet them, as a means of gaining significance. The price I pay in taking on too much responsibility is to lose time and space for myself. So when I listen to Morag I may over-emphasize the issues she shares that feel close to my heart, and unconsciously impose 'my way' of doing things, particularly at the reorientation phase. This will be a sure way of creating stuckness in our work. I will take this to supervision and perhaps later I will need to use immediacy and self-disclosure to address this if it does get in the way. Although I use self-disclosure sparingly, it can be helpful to model 'the courage to be imperfect'.

Staying with the counselling relationship, Morag's lifestyle suggests to me that she may wish to be the 'good client', while also being impatient if her issues are not rapidly resolved. The pull she experiences between a presentable sociable front and her underlying aggression may create a tension in therapy. This could result in her leaving therapy if we are not able to address this fairly early on. A clue for this comes when she says: 'when things don't go well, you start thinking that the grass is greener elsewhere'. As this is a central aspect of her lifestyle, I hope we can explore this usefully as she gains insight into her private logic.

If I am not sufficiently respectful, another area that could be a problem concerns her need to avoid self-exposure or show negative feelings. My sense is that if she fears being 'stripped bare' or 'found out' in the early sessions, she will become very defensive and shut down from gaining insight. Without wanting to protect or rescue her, I need to maintain empathy and a respectful pacing in putting my hypotheses to her, and also when working on issues likely to touch more painful emotions. I am very aware of the emotional power of processes such as art, imaging and psychodrama, and so will assess the situation carefully before introducing these in therapy.

Regarding her wish to 'rationalize her angry feelings', I will need to be careful to ensure our therapy goals are aligned. When Morag says of her aggression 'it's something one's got to get over', I reflect that it will be important to address the purpose of the angry feelings, and to help Morag give herself permission to experience the feelings, perhaps through the use of paradoxical intention. This may be counter to Morag's initial wants, and we will need to address this openly.

Morag spent a good bit of the first session sharing issues around her relationship with James. I sense that issues relevant to couples therapy may re-emerge, and I need to ensure I do not find myself pulled into working on James's issues rather than on Morag's. If this continues to happen, I will use immediacy, and perhaps put forward the idea of referral to a couples counsellor.

All the above issues could lead to stuckness and ineffective working practice on my part, and would need resolution. However, I am hopeful that with my own internal supervision, listening to the tapes, and my supervisor's overview, I can address these problem areas, and shift from stuckness.

When I began working using the Adlerian approach, I was far less flexible in the procedures I used. In my enthusiasm, I wanted to carry out full formal lifestyle assessment in the very early stages. While some people specifically request this, I feel this can be counterproductive with many clients. Despite the valuable insights lifestyle assessment can provide very rapidly, it is communicating these back effectively to the client that is the essential art. Adler could do this brilliantly in a brief single session. However, I am not Adler and need to be true to my own style and level of skill.

Criteria for successful outcome

This comparatively brief therapy input aims to help Morag challenge her mistaken ideas and unrealistic goals, and develop a growing sense of social interest. This process hopefully will continue long after Morag ends working with me. The therapy has an educative form, providing insights and strategies that can be used as a base for ongoing behaviour change in the future.

In broad terms, the criteria for a positive outcome for Morag are:

- to begin to modify her faulty perceptions of how she thinks she 'must' be, and appreciate that she has choice;
- to begin to put her insights into positive action;
- to feel she can contribute and cooperate with those around her, on an equal rather than competitive basis.

More specifically, Morag began the sessions stating that she wanted to work on her feelings of aggression, and to understand her desire for new challenge. I am confident that both these areas can be explored usefully following assessment of her lifestyle. I sense that Morag will be quick to gain insight into her private logic. As lifestyle work is about a holistic understanding of a person's movement through life, this will have application to all other areas Morag may wish to explore, such as her feelings around relationships, and the conflict between freedom and responsibility.

I feel that with the support and challenge of therapy, Morag will be ready to address her grief in the relationship with Carl, and by the end of our contract will have moved towards a resolution of this grief. The work around her relationship with James, although closely connected, feels larger. It touches very closely with the 'myself' or 'mother-hen' conflict, and as she begins to explore this it could feel threatening to the relationship in the short term. So it may be here, and perhaps in other areas, that Morag gains insight, but is not ready to act on the insight. This is fine. I will respect her right to choose when and how she changes, if at all. I do not see this as 'failure'; if therapy outcomes are assessed over too short a time, the long-term effects of her insights may be missed.

While we will keep to our clearly contracted ending, it may be that Morag contacts me again in the future. The space between therapy periods can be a fruitful time of consolidation and growth. The new therapy contract then offers a fresh focus, with new goals, that allows for further movement.

Summary

Coming to the end of this work, I am surprised to feel a realness in the relationship with Morag. The project feels both exciting and frustrating. My frustration lies largely in having to relate to Morag via the printed page, which I experienced as a barrier to the natural and creative flow of therapy. The therapy process is not one I plan in advance. I do have certain attitudes, skills and procedures that come with me into the therapy room. However, I see the creativity of therapy emerging from the interaction between us, as equals, each of us making equal, albeit different, contributions to the process. This involves enabling Morag to lead me where she needs to go, while I will also be encouraging her to go in directions that may be challenging, but can facilitate her insight and growth. This will only be effective if I pace the process appropriately and maintain respect.

Practising Adlerian therapy offers me a solid base structure and a flexibility which suits my own need for both containment and autonomy. (I can hear echoes of Morag here.) My therapeutic style may be very different from another Adlerian therapist, although we will share a holistic socio-teleological view of the person, and will work to understand the person's lifestyle. Looking to the immediate future in my practice, I envisage maintaining this Adlerian base, while continuing to learn from other approaches, particularly those that touch trans-personal and spiritual aspects of therapy.

Therapy is limited in what it can offer, and I do not see it as the panacea to everything. The aim of therapy with Morag is to enable her to have the courage to continue her personal growth within the community, dealing simultaneously with her inner and outer worlds.

Further reading

Adler, A. (1933). *Social Interest: A Challenge to Mankind*. London: Faber and Faber.
Adler, A. (1992a). *What Life Could Mean To You*. Oxford: One World.
Adler, A. (1992b). *Understanding Human Nature*. Oxford: One World.
Ansbacher, H.L. and Ansbacher, R.R. (eds) (1964). *The Individual Psychology of Alfred Adler*. New York: Harper and Row.
Clifford, J. (1990). Adlerian therapy. In W. Dryden (ed.), *Individual Therapy: A Handbook*. Buckingham: Open University Press.
Corey, G. (1991). *Theory and Practice of Counselling and Psychotherapy: Adlerian Therapy*, pp. 136–70. Pacific Grove, CA: Brooks/Cole.
Dreikurs, R. (1967). *Psychodynamics, Psychotherapy and Counselling: Collected Papers*. Chicago, IL: Alfred Adler Institute.
Manaster, G.J. and Corsini, R.J. (1982). *Individual Psychology: Theory and Practice*. Itasca, Illinois: F.E. Peacock.
Mosak, H. (1989). Adlerian psychotherapy. In *Current Psychotherapies*, 4th edn, pp. 65–116. Itasca, Illinois: F.E. Peacock.

PETER SAVAGE

(9)

HYPNOTHERAPY

The therapist

Much of my education and professional training was undertaken as
a mature student, following a variety of jobs including several years'
work overseas in both voluntary and paid posts. I consider the time
that I spent, amongst other things, travelling abroad working in
refugee camps, as a UN Consultant with the WHO's smallpox eradi-
cation programme, and other projects in Asia, an influential and
formative period in my life. A knowledge of the wider world before
undertaking higher education and embarking upon any career may
help ensure more objective choices and more fulfilling outcomes.
This is, perhaps, not least true in the case of psychotherapy. Following a conventional route, without pause – school/college, university,
professional training – may well produce an expensively trained,
relatively youthful, academic sharing little in common with, even
alienated from, the majority of the population; if only to recoup the
investment in time and money of the therapist's own training, he
or she may then cater solely, and at great therapeutic length, for the
needs of the wealthy. Since the great majority of people are, at best,
of modest means (a circumstance which, of itself, may promote or
exacerbate psychological distress), a popular therapy should be available. It needs to be relatively brief, non-dogmatic, yet with a long
history of success in use. Its practitioners, in short, should be PUPS
– pragmatic, utilitarian psychotherapists. Such considerations figured
amongst those which prompted my choosing to train as a hypnotherapist with the National College of Hypnosis and Psychotherapy,
subsequently joining the College's tutorial team, and becoming
Principal in 1987.

The College offers a rigorous training in classical and contemporary hypnotherapy, externally assessed and accredited. Its curriculum includes a study of various schools of psychological thought (which I chose to supplement with a study of Applied Psychology at Manchester University), considering varying views on the derivation and treatment of such problems as may be encountered in therapy. Hence, trainees may assess a similar presenting problem and its appropriate treatment from the contrasting viewpoints of, say, psychoanalysis and behaviourism. Importantly, the college does not say, 'Approach A is right, and approach B is wrong', but opts rather for saying, 'This is what adherents of approach A hold to be the case; and, conversely, this is what the supporters of approach B have to say on the matter. Having considered the arguments on both sides, what do you think?' The significance of this non-partisan attitude is that no single theoretical stance/clinical practice is imposed upon trainees and, by association, those who subsequently seek their help. Were our graduates dentists, therefore, their skills would include straightening, scaling, polishing and filling teeth, rather than, say, simply extracting.

Modern hypnotherapy derives from the eighteenth-century work of Mesmer and his followers (Buranelli 1976). Its development has been explored at length and in detail (Weitzenhoffer 1989), yet the medium through which it works, hypnosis, remains a matter for speculation and research (Rossi 1986/1993). Drawing upon this wealth of knowledge and theory, a contemporary hypnotherapy session might typically comprise the induction of the hypnotic state, treatment in hypnosis, and termination (Mallet 1989: 211–31). The therapist may talk to the subject about a narrowing of attention as external distractions are allowed to fade. (This is similar to everyday experiences, such as becoming engrossed in a book or film.) So, perhaps, the subject is encouraged to concentrate, eyes closed, on a growing sense of physical relaxation whilst other stimuli recede. The simple fact of eye-closure dramatically improves concentration by shutting out visual stimuli, and others, such as everyday sounds, become less intrusive, if noted at all. A well-motivated subject, confident in both therapy and therapist (criteria in which he or she may be educated in and out of hypnosis), is then receptive to any therapy, mutually agreed prior to commencement, intended to change behaviour, thought or feeling. (Isn't this reminiscent of how that intuitive hypnotherapist – the human mother – copes with distress in her children?) Given that imaginative involvement, selective attention and suspension of the critical process characterize the hypnotic state, any or all psychological techniques may be delivered via the hypnotic medium. The subject may relive and reinterpret negative past experiences and look into a positive future; practise coping techniques;

learn to correct thoughts and feelings inimical to emotional well-being, and behaviour harmful to physical health; reassess life's problems and reappraise its potential; master self-hypnosis as an aid to personal involvement in achieving the therapeutic aim. At termination, post-hypnotic suggestions relating to this same aim may be delivered, and the subject gently returned to the here-and-now. Subject and therapist then discuss the therapeutic experience with a view to informing and improving future therapy. In so doing, the therapist defers to the proper source of expertise and control which lies not with the therapist but the person in therapy.

Further information requested

Many of the questions that I asked of Morag had to do with determining whether or not hypnotherapy was contraindicated at all, or whether certain techniques would be contraindicated. Luckily, neither was the case, but it is worth spending some time looking at the sort of information required and obtained to satisfy me in these important areas. Morag was asked for details of her medical history and any medication. Other than two isolated attacks of migraine she has been in good health all her life. She keeps paracetamol as a stand-by in the event of any recurrence of the migraine, but has recourse to no other drugs. There is, therefore, no medical evidence that Morag suffers or has suffered any condition, such as clinical depression, which would require me to refer to her general practitioner, or other medical adviser. This same caution would need to be observed if the presenting problem might have been organic in origin. If, for example, Morag had been presenting with the migraine, I should have needed to be satisfied that her doctor had ruled out any physical cause, such as a brain tumour. Here, the ill-advised use of hypnosis might fatally delay the intervention of a surgeon.

Having confirmed that hypnotherapy is not contraindicated, I also checked for contraindications to any techniques which might be employed. Prior to eye-closure, for instance, I might have Morag gaze at a fixed point until at my suggestion, and as a consequence of the eye muscles tiring, her eyes close. Given her past history of migraine, I should be careful to avoid any fixed point likely to trigger an attack, such as a pinpoint of light. Other than the migraine, Morag has given me no reason to think that any technique we choose to induce and deepen the hypnotic state, and obtain responses in hypnosis if necessary, should be avoided. If I asked her to imagine herself in a garden, take some deep breaths, and give a slight finger movement to show how relaxed she felt, none of this would present a problem for her. Although none of these techniques is contraindicated, since Morag has no prior experience of hypnotherapy, precisely which would be best is a matter for discussion and testing in practice.

In addition to obtaining routine information of the kind discussed above, I was interested to learn more which might have a bearing on the therapy to be recommended. I wanted to know whether the presenting problem remained as before, whether Morag had any insight into its origin, and for how long it had troubled her. I wanted to know more about her personal background, family background, employment history, hobbies and interests. Does Morag have any views on the concept of an unconscious mind? What was her current stress/arousal level? Does she hyperventilate?

It seems that, as she perceives it, Morag's problem has worsened. The way in which Morag articulates the problem is laboured and imprecise. To my question, 'Does the presenting problem remain as described in the first session?', Morag replied:

> The conflict with James, and the conflict about, you know, my work as opposed to looking after the house, well sometimes I think it's even worse than it was before, in that I'm the . . . er . . . I'm not coping with work so well. I kind of feel I'm letting a lot of people down on that front as well. Um . . . so in a sense that's almost got worse. Um . . . as I say the children . . . I suppose I just feel that my feel that they've got bigger problems than my problems and I should you know, be doing . . . you know, it doesn't really matter, my problems sound niggly to maybe, the trauma they're going through.

This same difficulty in articulating her meaning was also encountered when Morag was asked whether she had any insight into the origin of the presenting problem:

> I . . . am really puzzled by, by my feelings towards James's ex-wife. I mean I've . . . [thinks] I don't know – the thoughts that I've had since, I don't know with Carl, for example, I don't know whether, I don't know whether the fact that my father had affairs with people, and it upset my mother – I mean, I don't know whether that's why I was not prepared to accept anybody that, you know, it's . . . that was deceitful. Um . . . I got a bit lost there.

Although asked it, Morag had nothing further to add to the subject of the possible origins of her presenting problem. Her next answer, though, ostensibly to do with the date from which she had become aware of the problem's existence, had more to do with origins:

I . . . when . . . when I had given up work at the City Council, so Jessica must be eighteen months old, so I was just starting on a new career, you know, kind of trying to get it together, then James said, 'Well, if you're working from home we can have the children to live with us'. Because his wife was going through this – well, first she said she wanted to go away to college, and then she wanted to do something else, and in the end – she ended up just having a nervous breakdown . . . and I guess I felt very trapped then, I think. You know, I couldn't . . . you know, I couldn't – well I suppose I could have said 'No', but because James had gone down the road that he'd sort of agreed to have a child, that he, you know, perhaps would really have preferred not to have had that sort of responsibility – I felt that I'd got to, you know, if his children needed looking after, I'd really got to do, you know, I'd got to do that for him. Um . . . I suppose, for the children really rather than for him. I guess I felt that he was, I felt that he was quite unfair to put it on me with a small child, and trying to work and everything as well. Um . . . and I think that's probably where I mean the whole, I suppose the whole thing with Paula [James's former wife] and whatever, you know, reared its head much more then and . . . I guess that – they did live with us for two years.

Morag's family background was, to her recollection, largely un-exceptional, although she suspected her father of having affairs which hurt her mother. She uses words like 'distant', 'unemotional', 'not very affectionate' of her father, while her mother was 'loving and cuddly'. She had generally good relations with an elder brother and sister, and one sister younger than her. Speaking of this period in her life, Morag describes it as: 'Happy. Yeah. Had an enjoyable childhood – there was always lots going on, and we laughed a lot'. The children were required to be polite and encouraged to be inde-pendent. Morag felt that a 'jobs rota' to be completed before they could go out to play on Saturdays was important in her develop-ment, and her father emphasized the value of 'stickability' – seeing any job though to completion once undertaken. As with her family background, Morag's employment history reveals nothing out of the ordinary in itself. Speaking of hobbies and interests, Morag says she would like to travel more, but in some ambiguous way: 'This is made more difficult, you know, with younger people . . .'. Perhaps the younger people are her daughter, and James's children.

Morag has no particular concept of the unconscious mind, had a high stress level at the time of the second interview and, seemingly, has a tendency to hyperventilate.

Assessment

I should think that some of Morag's childhood experiences have a bearing on her present difficulties. This is not to suggest that independence, say, is a negative quality in an individual. In Morag's instance, it was probably independence, self-discipline, sociability and other inherent and/or nurtured characteristics (including her father's ideal, 'stickability') which have helped her become a successful businesswoman. (To this list we might add the Adlerian concept of 'striving for superiority', given Morag's position in the family hierarchy.) On the other hand, Morag's having such qualities may have made her intolerant of those who, as she sees things, do not possess them. She may draw unfavourable comparisons between those who lack these qualities and those who have them. This becomes problematical when the individuals concerned have an impact on Morag's life. What might have been a source of minor irritation in a stranger becomes a source of resentment, provoking reactive anxiety, in persons closer to Morag. This anxiety and its effect manifest not only in the response to initial psychological testing, showing high stress and low arousal (Mackay *et al.* 1978: 283–4), but also in the hesitation and uncertainty which typify the interviews in parts. Leaving aside the single case of infidelity by her former partner, Carl, which reminded her so painfully of her father's infidelities, Carl and Morag seem to compare favourably with other persons cited in her two accounts. (It may be significant that the term 'love' is not employed when referring to Carl, or anybody else, although her mother was 'loving' and Morag would 'love to travel some more'.) As a result of this anxiety, Morag's work is suffering, probably in turn exacerbating dissatisfaction with her personal life, and vice versa, resulting in the classical 'vicious circle': somebody's personal life does not give satisfaction, that discontent reflects adversely in performance at work, that discontent at work is brought home, so aggravating domestic unhappiness, and so on.

Morag's childhood environment fostered a commitment to hard work, independence, sociability and 'stickability'. She had an elder brother whom she felt that her mother spoiled, and an older sister who 'could wind [her father] round her little finger'. It was Morag's mother who 'would encourage everybody to be as independent as they could', and her father who encouraged ' "stickability" and not giving up . . . playing a lot of games . . . a sort of ethic there that you strive to win'; and each child had his or her allotted domestic chores. Should anybody come to the family door, 'you always made them feel as welcome as possible . . . everybody enjoyed social occasions and talking'. In her subsequent life experience, Morag came across persons who lacked one or other, if not all, of these family values.

Morag's present partner, James, his children and former wife do not appear in a favourable light. The children 'don't help us with anything', and the boy is 'particularly selfish'. The children need only enter Morag's house for her to feel aggressive. As for their mother, 'her name only has to be mentioned and I can feel myself inside sort of knotting up'. Unlike Morag, Paula is 'pretty hopeless. She works for a couple of hours a week, and her father's firm pays an extortionate amount for the amount that she does'. This hopelessness resulted in Morag's having to take in Paula's two children when Morag's own child was very young, and Morag was struggling to establish her business. Morag had to undertake the additional responsibility simply because Paula 'couldn't cope with them', and following pressure from James which she resented, a resentment fed by his perceived lack of affection for their own child and, unlike Morag, not wanting another: 'I would probably have liked another child, but I think James didn't really want . . . it was a bit of a protest for him to accept the one in the first place'. Whilst Morag describes herself as 'a very practical person, somebody that just gets on with things', Paula 'doesn't know what she's doing or whatever'. Morag admits to being, 'probably selfish', but there is no doubt in her mind that Paula is 'a very selfish person [who] doesn't do anything if it doesn't suit her to do it'.

James (and others, Morag suspects) has found it very exhausting trying to keep up with her. She finds relaxation and challenge in doing something totally different, hence the second of her businesses, which James did not encourage 'because he felt it would take a lot of time away from him'; but this has been so successful that Morag now indicates a wish 'to do something else!'. (I feel that if Morag had not put in the exclamation mark, James might have requested it.) Given this creative ambition, Morag finds mundane housework irksome and resents James wanting her to be at home 'because his children are there'. Morag enjoys all aspects of business, while James (working for his former father-in-law) does not enjoy his work. Were Morag in that position, she would change her job, and is frustrated by James not doing so. While his work leaves little energy for free time activities, I wonder whether there is some sexual metaphor in Morag's complaining that James 'tends to flop at the weekend'.

Whatever may be the case, I do not find Morag's commitment to the relationship convincing ('I'm fairly determined that I want this relationship to stay') and there seems to be many strains on it. Amongst other things she is too independent for him, does more for his children than he, considers his watching television a total waste of time, and is not tidy enough around the house. To overcome this last difficulty, Morag has established a separate living area at the top of the house for herself and for her daughter – a child he did not want but Morag insisted upon.

When referring to a youthful marriage, Morag says 'I felt I'd got the wrong person, that we weren't really compatible'; and, ominously, 'he's more or less much the same as James'. By contrast, the relationship Morag enjoyed (I use the word advisedly) before James seemed much more fulfilling. It foundered because of a single infidelity on Carl's part, when Morag had hoped to marry and have children with him. They enjoyed talking to each other, discussing work, entertaining, and 'Carl would put as many ideas into the relationship as I would. It was an interesting time'. My impression is that none of this would describe Morag's relationship with James, and Morag seems to sense an unconscious significance in the comparison of the two relationships: 'at the back of my mind comparing it to when I used to live with Carl . . . maybe that's there in my subconscious . . . maybe that is affecting me, my life without him [Carl]'. At the second interview, when checking for habits which often betray hyperventilation (Lum 1977: 7–11; Wilkinson 1988: 115–25), one such habit – sighing – is more noticeable when Morag talks of Carl. Since we already have some indication of hyperventilation from a standard test noting whether breathing is predominantly upper chest or abdominal – the former indicating hyperventilation – the sighing is probably emotional in origin.

At the initial interview, the interviewer noted that, following a fluent start and without much obvious feeling, Morag's account became hesitant, with regular rephrasing and changes of direction. These mannerisms typified the second interview also. I believe this to be indicative of reactive anxiety as the interviews touched upon emotionally charged areas. She is, rather guiltily, resentful of James's ex-wife and children, and unhappy with James whom she compares unfavourably with Carl, towards whom her feelings are uncertain. The conflicts thus aroused are having a detrimental effect upon her work. Since it is that work and her own child which have the major claim to her affections, Morag might be happy to confine her energies to them, at least for the present. All of this will need checking out, since I can only surmise, and only Morag can know.

Therapeutic possibilities

It used to be thought that hypnotherapy could only be successful if the subject were unintelligent and weak-willed. The therapist was supposed to impose his or her will on the subject, who was merely the passive recipient of suggestion, willy-nilly. Such is not the credo of modern hypnotherapy, which holds that virtually anyone may derive benefit from this form of therapy, assuming that three criteria are present: that the subject wants, expects and allows the therapy to succeed. It might be objected that, say, somebody who presented with a smoking problem would fulfil all of these criteria. Yet, despite the report of a meta-analysis of anti-smoking therapies showing hypnotherapy to be the most successful (Matthews 1992: 6), some people continue to smoke despite such therapy. Allowing for indifferent technique or other incompetence on the part of the therapist, how then do we account for the 'failures'? Returning to the three criteria, if, when the subject says 'I want to stop smoking' what he or she really should have said is 'My wife/husband/workmates/society at large, want me to stop smoking', then the element of personal volition is missing. By association, the other criteria of expectation and consent are wanting and a successful outcome less likely. In some instances, the therapist may then be blamed for the 'failure', when the individual concerned had no intention of quitting.

The trivialization of hypnosis for purposes of entertainment is probably much to blame for misconceptions about hypnotherapy, which may deter people who might otherwise benefit from therapy. Quite often, such entertainers may be proponents of the serious applications of hypnosis in therapy, but undermine such advocacy in their own choice of its use. Whether the application be serious or otherwise, however, the three criteria remain: the therapist's subject, or stage hypnotist's volunteer, should want, expect and allow hypnosis to take place.

A further consideration is that because hypnotherapy is a cooperative endeavour, the (usually) two participants must want to work together. Morag should want to work with me, and I with her. There may be something in one or other of us which is 'off-putting', so that through no fault on either side Morag might do better to be referred to one of my colleagues. Nothing that I know of Morag to date would suggest that I would not want to work with her, and I shall hope that she feels the same towards me. Also, and most importantly, I feel competent to help in Morag's instance, not only by virtue of my training but because I am attracted by the challenge of the problems presented.

Until we meet, I must assume that Morag fulfils the criteria to which I refer above. Certainly, she displays other characteristics which are most promising in therapeutic terms. She has intelligence and determination, qualities which would help militate towards success in virtually any therapy. In terms of hypnotherapy, in particular, Morag has the ability to become imaginatively involved: 'I . . . read a book, and get totally immersed in that'. This quality – absorption – is common in childhood, but often reduces as we grow older. It is generally agreed that this is one of the qualities which help make children the best subjects for hypnosis. It follows, therefore, that those who are able to bring forward the quality into adulthood will make good hypnotic subjects. They may concentrate on the problem in hand to the exclusion of extraneous distractions, with excellent prospects for a successful outcome. In my own instance, as a child my mother's reassuring presence and suggestions were capable of banishing any hurt, physical or emotional. Although Morag has said that she has no prior experience of hypnotherapy, I understand this to mean in the formal sense. Her account of her relationship with her mother suggests that she was just as much a primitive hypnotherapist as most mothers. I am confident, too, that Morag has a similar relationship with her own daughter. Hence, Morag has both experienced and used positive suggestion to advantage. She would, therefore, be entering therapy with a confidence established by personal precedent.

The course of therapy

In this instance, I should approach therapy in three different, but concurrent, ways, and add a fourth approach with input from another source. This all assumes Morag's agreement. I should wish to ensure that Morag is able to make a clear distinction between being tense and being relaxed; that she corrects any tendency to hyperventilate; that she becomes, habitually, mentally calm, physically relaxed and confident. Adjunctive to this therapy, I shall recommend that Morag consult a Relate – or similarly trained – counsellor.

Morag has displayed tension on more than one occasion at both interviews to date. Her interviewer has reported that Morag's voice cracks and that she is tearful at certain times. Tension existed in her family background, when she was aware of arguments between her parents, and she was distressed by her father's infidelity and its effect on her mother. She had a failed marriage while still a student and her subsequent relationships have not been easy. Her former work, and present self-employment as she copes with a young child, must have put a strain upon her. In such circumstances, it will not be surprising to find that Morag is habitually tense, and has lost the ability to distinguish that state from a feeling of relaxation. Also, when at rest, her breathing is thoracic, rather than abdominal; this is indicative of hyperventilation, commonly associated with anxiety, although the connection is not always made. Because of this, the simple corrective treatment may not be undertaken, and the condition will persist with the consequent adverse physical effects compounding the psychological condition.

It is not impossible to expect that correcting habitual tension and hyperventilation, alone, may signal the end of therapy. This will depend upon Morag, and whether any specific therapeutic goals are to be set. In popular contemporary terms, Morag may be described as suffering stress. This has to do with her appraisal of how well, or ill, she is able to adjust to the demands of her environment (Lazarus 1966; Cox 1985: 1155–63). Morag is therefore the judge, although perhaps we shall agree specific tests to confirm her success in any such 'environmental adjustment' (e.g. her post-therapy rating of how she feels towards events and individuals which formerly caused notable distress).

Assuming that Morag's distress is not dissipated as a 'by-product', as it were, of the approaches mentioned above, I shall recommend either cognitive behavioural therapy, within the hypnotic medium (Golden *et al.* 1987: 51–4), or direct suggestion via hypnosis. (Since a cognitive behavioural method is discussed elsewhere in this book, I shall describe the direct suggestion method here, and later a self-monitoring method derived from the same.) Either method would seem to fit Morag's case, since she is able to identify the sources of her distress. In hypnosis, too, we may explore Morag's wish 'to understand why I enjoy doing things. I enjoy challenges ... Is it right that I should always be wanting something new to go at, some new challenge? Should I just be accepting the way I am?' What is required therefore is to ensure that such stressors cease to cause the level of distress currently reported. This adjustment, once achieved, will allow Morag to function more efficiently, making decisions in her personal and business life conducive to harmony in both.

I make the recommendation that a specialist counsellor should also be consulted because I do not have the appropriate training, and Morag's personal relationships seem central to her difficulties. In particular, Morag is troubled by the situation with James (and its satellite problems over his former wife and their children) and seems unclear in her feelings towards him and her former partner, Carl. It is strange that Morag does not remember whether it was James or Carl who insisted that she choose between them when she was going out with both. That choice, however, was made in favour of James 'probably before I was ready'.

We are all regularly exhorted to relax in a variety of circumstances. At the doctor's, for instance, we are told to 'Just relax', as the doctor does not quite conceal a hypodermic syringe with a needle half the length of the street outside; at the dentist's, we are invited to relax whilst contemplating a set of tools apparently borrowed from men who have been repairing that same street! There is a very good reason for this, since the pain is greater if the muscles are tense. (Check this, by pinching a fold of skin on the back of your open, relaxed, hand and then tensing the muscles by clenching the fist. Imagine the effect on the whole body if much of its musculature is tense over extended periods.) However, we may as well be told to 'Just speak Serbo-Croat' or 'Just fly this aeroplane' if we have not learned to do what we are asked. Morag's learning to appreciate (in all senses) relaxation will be simple, although best practised in privacy, unless she also wants to use the skill for instance to clear space for herself on crowded public transport. She must practise tensing, and then very slowly relaxing, various muscle groups throughout her body, face included. In this way, she will soon appreciate the distinction between the two opposite conditions, recognizing unnecessary tension whenever it occurs and dispelling it by relaxing.

Morag will also learn to change from thoracic to abdominal breathing. Lounging in a chair with her right hand, say, on the upper chest, and the left on the navel, her breathing should be such that she should observe greater movement of the left hand. Morag must be encouraged to breathe slowly and rhythmically, pausing and relaxing before breathing in and allowing the in-breath to change smoothly into the out-breath, pausing and relaxing, again, at completion of the exhalation, and so on. Her breathing rate should slow to six to eight breaths a minute at rest. Given practice – ten to twenty minutes twice a day – these improved breathing techniques will become habitual and automatic, whether at rest or engaged in everyday activities. Since anxiety has been linked to incorrect breathing, and vice versa, and the two have been linked to ill health overall, Morag's new skills will promote physical and psychological well-being.

We shall tackle Morag's specific problems by suggestion in hypnosis. Suggestion, alone, is very powerful as witnessed by the multi-million pound advertising industry; for whatever reason, it is yet more powerful, and quick-acting, when combined with hypnosis. The would-be non-smoker, for instance, knows all of the reasons – health, financial, social – to cease smoking. Quite often, though, it is only reiteration of these reasons through suggestion in hypnosis which helps end the behaviour. Morag is seemingly aware of those aspects of her life which cause distress, in whatever form. By suggestion, in hypnosis she will learn to cope with such stressors, remaining mentally calm, physically relaxed and confident. It is important, though, that realistic suggestions be made. To do otherwise would be to insult Morag's intelligence, and adversely affect the therapy. Hence, I shall not suggest, for instance, that persons, events and situations will never upset Morag again, but rather that their power to upset will diminish. Concurrently, Morag's power to confront – but not exaggerate – life's problems will be enhanced. I shall supplement our weekly therapy sessions with a tailor-made therapy tape for Morag to play daily. Given her wish always to be tackling something new though, Morag will need little encouragement from me to be taught self-hypnosis. By this medium, she will avoid undesirable dependence upon the therapist.

I shall not make any contract with Morag other than mutually to agree a review after (say) six therapy sessions. At that stage, Morag will have the opportunity to assess progress to date and decide perhaps whether to continue in therapy. Morag may opt to remain in therapy, but that the therapy take a different direction. In addition to coping with stress, she may wish to explore what underlies it. Some such insight may have emerged, although not deliberately sought, at the sessions already completed, including counselling sessions if undertaken.

Problem areas

I should consider problem areas a misnomer if a different direction in therapy were indicated as a result of insight. Problems would include whether rapport exists between Morag and me, whether Morag is committed to therapy, whether there is any impediment to the therapy proposed, or techniques intended, and all such issues have been addressed above. In the course of therapy, though, material may be uncovered which might seemingly present a problem, but in reality provides an opportunity.

The origins of Morag's distress appear self-evident, so a mastery of coping techniques, along with counselling, will reduce or remove its detrimental effect upon her life. Apart from the specific stressors already identified, Morag's distress is heightened by her partner's criticism. I attach importance to when the criticism is delivered too: 'he'd criticize just before we go to bed at night, which is obviously when you're at your weakest and lowest. And he'd almost pick a fight'. Many therapists consider sleep to be an excellent addendum to therapy. The sleeping hours, preceded by an individually made audio-tape, can extend therapy effortlessly into a medium, the potentialities of which continue to excite research (LaBerge and Rheingold 1990). Add to this the concept that we all regularly enter trance states akin to hypnosis (Rossi 1986/1993) and an unfortunate precedent typifies Morag's situation. Whereas in sleep Morag might rehearse positive therapy and look to a fruitful outcome, a fight with James is more likely to precipitate recreation and multi-sensory accessing of past unhappiness with ever more corrosive effects upon the relationship.

All these factors, with the presenting problem apparently a combination of obviously unfortunate causes and inevitable unhappy effects, have prompted the choice of therapy described. Yet Morag herself has presentiments of something more profound. She uses phrases like 'at the back of my mind', 'maybe that's there in my subconscious', 'maybe I should do a bit of exorcism'. Obviously, these may be merely expressions of speech, not indicative of Morag's belief in anything other than the conscious mind and everyday world. Indeed, when asked if such terms as 'subconscious' or 'unconscious' had any significance for her, Morag did not even remember using the former: 'I've used that, do they say? . . . er . . . I don't know . . .'. However, there may be a significance in someone's use of language beyond that apparently intended. Someone may use the term 'mesmerized', for instance, without knowing its origin, or without recognizing how easily he or she can enter the hypnotic state. Morag's use of near-analytic expressions may imply some inkling of an unconscious motivation for her behaviour. The second interview revealed that Morag had followed a counselling course for two years. It is quite likely that she would have been exposed to psychodynamic theories at that time.

Because of this, and without specific intent, Morag may access material to which no allusion is made in therapy, and its concomitant emotion. Whether direct suggestion is used (e.g. 'so, little by little, yet with gathering pace, you will find that your troubles are receding into the past') or indirect suggestion, where I may draw Morag's attention to a natural object, the characteristics of which Morag may benefit from emulating (e.g. 'consider an oak tree, sturdy yet graceful, capable of resisting the vicissitudes of nature'), the result may go beyond the intention. Merely referring to the past may inadvertently put Morag in mind of some event in the past: the oak tree may put her in mind of some long-forgotten incident. Even my tone of voice, or a turn of phrase, may awaken some recollection for Morag which suggests that her presenting problems are symptomatic of some underlying psychological origin deserving exploration. If we accept this formulation, Morag's presenting problems are the occasionally triggered emotional manifestations of a past event, lost to Morag's conscious memory.

Some would hold that we must now help Morag in an attempt to recover the lost material – and hypnosis would be an appropriate medium for this purpose (Golden *et al.* 1987: 54–7) – and, to use her term, 'exorcize' it. (In therapeutic terms, I would rephrase this as reliving and re-enacting an event so traumatic as to have been banished from Morag's everyday memory, an understanding of which will explain its remaining emotional component as manifest in her presenting problem.) To do other than this, it is argued, would simply be to risk 'symptom substitution', whereby surface symptoms of some underlying psychological origin are removed, resulting in a remanifestation in an even more threatening form. By contrast, eminent authorities with many years of clinical experience (Hartland 1971: 194–7; Pratt *et al.* 1988: 119–20) attach little weight to this hypothesis.

Morag and I would need to discuss the implications of any such development, taking account of arguments for and against the existence of unconscious motivation. Basically, some theorists believe in an 'unconscious', while others do not, or at least claim it is not proven. Perhaps most people take a more pragmatic line, until such time as the argument may be resolved one way or another. To paraphrase the fictional detective Sherlock Holmes, they might say, 'When you have eliminated the impossible, whatever remains, however improbable, for the sake of convenience, we shall label the unconscious'. Fortunately, hypnotherapy has the techniques to accommodate whichever views Morag may hold.

Criteria for successful outcome

Morag will determine the criteria for 'success' and decide how far they are met. It is she who knows how she feels, in a general sense as well as in those particular situations which she has reported as stress-provoking. Therefore, we shall rely upon her subjective reports, much as would a medical practitioner in asking a patient about physical health, while continuing to monitor that outward manifestations do not contradict subjective report. (If, for example, Morag described herself as feeling relaxed while showing physical signs of being tense, this anomaly would need to be noted and explored. Some therapists might recommend measurement of physiological stress responses in any case, but this could introduce a complicating and unreliable dimension, as witness the 'lie detector' controversy in the USA.) We are all generally able to distinguish feeling well from not feeling well. In Morag's instance, relaxation training and therapy overall will have heightened this ability. What we need is some means of establishing grades of 'feeling well' by which the efficacy of the therapeutic process may be judged, continuously, from the outset of therapy.

One such approach would be to use a scale with '0' representing absence of anxiety and '100' maximum anxiety. Such an instrument – a Subjective Units of Discomfort Scale (SUDS) – will be used initially to confirm Morag's ability to relax when confronted with regular daily stressors. As the name of the instrument suggests, ratings depend upon self-report, though some discussion may be needed to make them meaningful. To look for a '0' rating while undertaking everyday activities, for instance, would mean being at risk when even crossing the road. With practice, Morag should be capable of maintaining a realistic normal level of between 25–35 SUDS (Golden *et al.* 1987: 48).

This approach is derivative of work on systematic desensitization and reciprocal inhibition (Wolpe 1958). In very general terms, condition 'A' inhibits the coexistence of condition 'B'. Morag's therapy has been aimed specifically at learning how to respond in a relaxed manner to situations which had previously aroused anxiety – effectively, to 'unlearn' her earlier anxious response. Hence, in Morag's instance, a sense of relaxation will replace anxiety, rather than the reverse. In the course of therapy, however, we have been aiming for a generalized sense of well-being, as well as Morag's being more comfortable in those particular situations which she has identified as stressful. In the previous paragraph, a method of measuring success in the general round of daily activities has been described. We can apply the same instrument to measure success in given situations.

We shall establish a hierarchy with SUDS ratings being attributed to specific anxiety-provoking events in Morag's experience. Hence, for example, waking on the morning of an anticipated visit from James's former wife and children will be at the lower end of the scale (25 SUDS), through various gradations, including preparing food (30 SUDS), tidying the house (35 SUDS), etc., to the visit itself at the higher end of the scale (90 SUDS). While relaxed in hypnosis, Morag will be invited to visualize the least anxiety-provoking event and so on up the scale until she senses the onset of heightened anxiety (signalled by a simple prearranged finger movement). Here a halt is made, and Morag is helped to return to the relaxed state by suggestion, or she returns herself to that state using the techniques she has learned. When therapy is resumed, it will be at a stage below which the onset of anxiety was evinced, perhaps starting at the bottom of the hierarchical ladder again. In this way, Morag will practise, in her imagination confronting and coping with those events that have caused distress. Her success will be signalled by her being able to sustain the same relaxed response when confronting those same events in reality. Effectively, positive suggestion will have replaced the negative, which has so damaging an effect on all our lives.

Summary

Throughout our contact, both the course of treatment and methods employed will be a matter for discussion and mutual decision. I shall review continuously what I am doing and how, informed not only by Morag's comments but also by input from professional colleagues with whom I shall discuss the work, whilst not breaching confidentiality. The exception to this confidentiality rule, with Morag's consent, would be the specialist counsellor I referred to above, if Morag has seen fit to follow my recommendation. In this instance, consultation would be aimed at shaping the course of therapy, and counselling, in whatever manner is consistent with desirable outcome. That anybody should come to a therapist should be a humbling experience for the therapist concerned. The therapist should repay the confidence displayed by assuring maximum care. Such care should include recognition of personal limitations, and referral where appropriate.

Morag is unhappy with the way things are now, and we must look to promoting favourable change. In the course of this change, we must recognize that its necessary components – personal insight and the resulting ways of looking at the outside world – may not be without distress in themselves and in the choices with which Morag is then confronted. However, given improvement in the associated phenomena of behaviour, thought and feeling, Morag will now have the resources to make informed choices, and cope with their associated effects.

Short of drastic surgery, or the like, it is not within anybody's power to take away the pain of what is now yesterday, and the fear of all tomorrows. I do feel confident, though, that by working together Morag can be reconciled to what is past, and look to the future with optimism.

Further reading

Buranelli, V. (1976). *The Wizard from Vienna*. London: Peter Owen Ltd.
Cox, T. (1985). The nature and measurement of stress. *Ergonomics*, Vol. 28.
Golden, W.L., Dowd, T.E. and Friedberg, F. (1987). *Hypnotherapy: A Modern Approach*. Oxford: Pergamon Press.
Hartland, J. (1971). *Medical and Dental Hypnosis and Its Clinical Applications*, 2nd edn. London: Baillière Tindall.
LaBerge, S. and Rheingold, H. (1990). *Exploring the World of Lucid Dreaming*. New York: Ballantine Books.
Lazarus, R.S. (1966). *Psychological Stress and the Coping Process*. New York: McGraw-Hill.
Lum, L.C. (1977). Breathing exercises in the treatment of hyperventilation and chronic anxiety states. *Chest, Heart and Stroke Journal*, Vol. 2, No. 1.
Mackay, C., Cox, T., Burrows, G. and Lazzerini, T. (1978). An inventory for the measurement of self-reported stress and arousal. *British Journal of Social and Clinical Psychology*, Vol. 17.
Mallet, J.E. (1989). Hypnosis and stress, prevention and treatment applications. In G.S. Everly (ed.), *A Clinical Guide to the Treatment of the Human Stress Response*. New York: Plenum Press.
Matthews, R. (1992). How one in five have given up smoking. *The New Scientist*, Vol. 136, p. 1845.
Pratt, G.J., Wood, D.P. and Alman, B.M. (1988). *A Clinical Hypnosis Primer*. New York: John Wiley.
Rossi, E. (1986). *The Psychobiology of Mind–Body Healing*. New York: Norton (revised edn, 1993).
Wallace, B. (1981). *Applied Hypnosis: An Overview*. Chicago, IL: Nelson-Hall.
Waxman, D. (1989). *Hartland's Medical and Dental Hypnosis*, 3rd edn. London: Baillière Tindall.
Weitzenhoffer, A.M. (1989). *The Practice of Hypnotism: Vol. 1: Traditional and Semi-traditional Techniques and Phenomenology; Vol. 2: Applications of Traditional and Semi-traditional Hypnotism. Non-traditional Hypnotism*. New York: John Wiley.
Wilkinson, J.B. (1988). Hyperventilation control techniques in combination with self-hypnosis for anxiety management. In M. Heap (ed.), *Hypnosis: Current Clinical, Experimental and Forensic Practices*. London: Croom Helm.
Wolpe, J. (1958). *Psychotherapy by Reciprocal Inhibition*. Stanford, CA: Stanford University Press.

MOIRA WALKER AND MORAG

REVIEW AND RESPONSE

The first two books in this series (Peta and Charlie) have both expressed the editors' gratitude to the therapists taking part, and I repeat those sentiments here. In the final stage of our contact, as Morag and I responded to the various contributors, I was once again impressed by the care and thoroughness of the therapists. My thanks go to them all. Although some have acknowledged or commented on the obvious limitations of a project of this nature – and it must be frustrating for those used to working face-to-face to have to work through the intermediary of the editors – nevertheless, they have shared with us valuable insights into their particular approaches to therapy.

As readers will see, some fascinating comparisons can be made between these different ways of conceptualizing and understanding one client's story. This would not have been possible without the therapists being prepared openly and generously to share their work: they have all put their work on the line. As the Introduction explains, the contribution on psychodrama was initially undertaken by Michael Watson. I had greatly enjoyed working with him in the early stages. Morag and I, with Michael Jacobs as recorder of the social atom exercise, found it very involving. We were very saddened to hear shortly afterwards of his death, and I am very grateful to Paul Holmes for taking over the chapter – not an easy task at that stage.

As with the other books in this series, this last chapter is written in conjunction with the client. As the contributions were received from the therapists they were sent to Morag. When she had had time to read them, we met together for a period of several hours split over two days to explore and review her responses. There is no significance to the order the therapists are presented below, other than that this was the order in which Morag discussed them. She made it clear that she found all the responses interesting and informative and that they all provided her with food for thought: they all had something to say that was of value. But it was also clear that some resonated with her more than others.

In drawing together this overview, and incorporating Morag's comments, space does not permit all the comparisons she made. Readers will doubtless be able to make their own.

Windy Dryden

Windy Dryden describes himself as representing rational emotive behaviour therapy (REBT), having initially trained in person-centred counselling. He then tried but rejected a psychodynamic approach. The approach is based on the premiss that irrational beliefs are at the core of psychological difficulties, and the focus is therefore on challenging and shifting these beliefs. The concept of the Therapeutic Alliance and social learning theory are key to his approach. Goals and tasks are central in his work and the therapy has a very definite focus, in that respect making it similar to Roxanne Agnew's expressive psychotherapy; there are nonetheless considerable differences. Some readers may be surprised to see the term 'core conditions' appear, being more familiar with this in terms of person-centred therapy. Similarly, 'actualizing' is a term used in a similar way to 'self-actualization' in person-centred therapy.

Dryden is the only therapist to express concern that Morag's partner was not to be involved in the project, and did not know about it. Morag commented on his concern over her partner:

> I do know what Windy Dryden means when he quotes
> somebody on what it can do if someone is left out. But
> James has a tremendous hate of counsellors and therapists,
> so I do wonder if it could achieve anything beneficial if he
> were to come along or be involved.

This raises interesting questions about when and whether to work conjointly. It also raises other questions.

There are many reasons for a client to want to keep their own therapy as their own private business and not share it with their partner, especially if their partner is likely to be hostile to it, and yet it is important to the client to seek help. Certainly, many clients would feel it is up to them to decide for themselves when this may be appropriate. Therapy may result in the ending of a relationship, but it may do just the opposite. Is the therapist to decide when an ending is desirable (for instance, leaving a violent relationship) and when it is not? To what extent should the therapist be concerned if a client's partner does not know about the therapy, if that relationship is a focus in the work? And is this still an issue when the relationship is *not* the central issue? Where is the line, and how do therapists draw it? Should the outcome of therapy, if it involves a major life decision for the client, be seen as an adult choice that the client is responsible for?

Windy Dryden draws our attention to a novel of Fay Weldon's, which is generally viewed as being strongly anti-therapy: it expresses a highly personal view, perceiving the therapy of one partner as a primary factor in the break-up of the relationship. Perhaps one novel should not be given too much power and influence, and certainly not generalized from; there are many novels I object to, or personally consider not worth the paper they are written on. I do not, as a result, damn all novelists. Dryden's concern gives rise to these questions and it is important that therapists consider them.

Dryden asked Morag to complete a range of questionnaires, noting that he would not normally ask clients to complete so many. What is not clear from this is whether he would normally use some questionnaires as a matter of usual procedure, as other therapists of a cognitive orientation often do (in this series, for example, see Ormrod in *Peta* and Ryle in *Charlie*). However it is interesting to note that in the absence of a face-to-face interview, he chose this method of eliciting information, the only one of the six therapists here to do so. In an earlier volume, Peta had been most dismissive of questionnaires, and Morag too was not enthusiastic about them. She found them difficult to complete, although she could also see that this does not invalidate their use:

> They were a pain, but whether that's because they make you think about things that you don't like to think about, I don't know. It was very time-consuming and it took hours; it couldn't be rushed off in an odd half-hour. Some of the questions I had to come back to having thought about them. There were some questions that I left because I didn't want to answer them and then I thought I'd better because I'm meant to have filled these in. Some of them are very difficult because nothing down there really feels to fit and yet there is some sort of obligation to answer.

Some therapists feel that completing questionnaires not only provides valuable insights into the client, but helps socialize the client into the therapeutic process, but in the above comments Morag usefully draws attention to the dilemma should a client not want to answer, or be puzzled by the questions.

She found Dryden's acknowledgement of the significance of guilt, and his questions and comments in that area, useful:

> His differentiation between different forms of guilt was useful, as this has possibly been part of the problem. I would need him to explain more about that, as I didn't always understand what he was really saying, and it seemed to be the crux of what he was trying to get at.

Dryden himself had expressed frustration at not being able to communicate accurately what he meant to Morag, and doubtless in a real session with her would have checked that she understood. It does, however, raise other questions for therapists to consider more generally: Do they use jargon without always realizing it? Do they confound their clients with incomprehensible language? Can clients reasonably be expected to question or challenge this, or should therapists check and monitor this themselves ?

In Dryden's assessment of Morag, he identifies an essential clash between the side of her that seeks challenge and the side of her that has a keen sense of responsibility. This is further compounded by her high expectations of herself and others. Morag felt this to be very accurate and pertinent:

> I thought that phrases like 'struggling to reconcile the strong desire for seeking challenges on the one hand with her responsibilities towards others on the other' seemed to me to epitomize what it is about. He has caught something there. He seemed to understand the problem.

Accurate assessment is clearly a very important aspect of REBT and it is essential that the client understands the difference between the two types of negative emotions and the two types of beliefs. The necessity of assessment being based on concrete examples of these concerns points to a major difference between this approach and others in this volume. It is firmly based in the reality of what is happening in the here-and-now. In terms of Morag's suitability for REBT, Dryden assesses this on the basis of an Opinion about Psychological Problems questionnaire. This suggests that Morag would prefer an active behavioural intervention, although she has a slight preference for psychodynamic and humanistic explanations of her psychological problems. This seems an accurate reflection of Morag's opinion, as did his acknowledgement that she may react strongly against an approach that might suggest she was irrational:

> Yes, there is an appeal to me in the problem-solving
> approach that takes things step by step. I do hate to be
> called irrational, so I know what he meant when he made
> his comment about that: maybe for the reason that he said,
> that women are often labelled as irrational. Words become
> misused.

However, although she felt there was a very definite appeal in an active model that focused specifically on agreed problem areas, and found the initial short-term contract attractive, there were other areas of her self that she feared might be overlooked in this approach:

> I felt his picking up the 'shoulds' was helpful. But I did also
> think that this approach was less good at allowing me to
> feel. I'm not sure where how you feel fits in and that's a bit
> worrying. If you explain away the 'shoulds' and the 'mights'
> it doesn't get to the core of what is inside.

Morag also appreciated Dryden's recognition that she may prefer to see a woman. Her response is interesting. She seems to feel that in this particular approach, with its emphasis on rationality, that it would not really matter:

> He picked up whether there would be problems because he's
> a male therapist. In some senses that possibly wouldn't
> bother me too much because I've worked with men before.
> On the one hand, one is more used to pouring everything
> out to female friends; but I regard this approach as a rational
> way forward, as something I've got to do some work on.
> Taking that approach, I don't think it would bother me.

She is clearly positive in many ways about this therapist:

> I did warm to him because I felt I knew where I was with
> him. As I've said I had reservations, but I thought that I
> could possibly work with him as at least this would be a
> starting point I could go from.

In terms of successful outcome, Dryden would develop a list of problems and goals accompanied by a rating scale to be completed by the client. So although Dryden acknowledges that success is difficult to quantify, this method does attempt to measure this.

Paul Holmes

Michael Watson, and Paul Holmes who completed the work for this chapter, shared much in their training and their development as psychodramatists, although Holmes comments that as therapists and authors there were differences in style between them. Paul Holmes takes his style from that created by the Morenos and integrates insights from other sources. He senses a conflict within himself between a somewhat aloof analytic stance, and being more real and available as a psychodramatist, pointing to an interesting stylistic difference between the two.

The social atom test, which gave Morag valuable insights, is aimed at helping clients to express visually and actively how they feel about important people in their lives. At another level, it helps the therapist to gain insight into the intra-psychic roots of the problem. Morag was extremely positive about participating in this exercise:

> I positively enjoyed doing the chair exercise, and I still think back to it at certain times. It put a lot of things in place. Its impact was that I could see my life at a scan and it was very interesting to me to see the balance between the love you have for someone and the responsibility that gives you, and the feeling of wariness it gives you, because you almost don't get one without the other. And I think it brought home to me the weight of responsibility for other people that I feel, but at the same time the support network of the friends that I have around me. I frequently think about that and it makes me feel stronger. It depicted things very powerfully, possibly because I'm a visual person. I did enjoy that. It was very useful, and even if no more came out of that approach, then that was a useful insight.

Having read my account of the social atom test, Paul Holmes picks up on Morag's 'ambivalent' relationship with her father and also comments on other key relationships in her life: with her stepchildren, her mother and her daughter. There is a noticeable difference in emphasis from Windy Dryden's approach, which does not explore past relationships in her family of origin. In terms of Holmes's assessment of Morag and her difficulties, another stark contrast to Dryden emerges: he explains that intake interviews, histories and questionnaires are not generally seen as helpful in this approach. Rather, what is relevant will be revealed in and through the psychodramatic action.

By definition, psychodrama is a form of group therapy, although there is one initial individual meeting with the therapist. This does not follow a set pattern: Holmes describes himself as going with the flow and energy of the person. This reflects the philosophy that is central to this whole therapeutic venture: the client controls and decides what is explored. Holmes feels confident that this type of therapy would be suitable for Morag. She was less sure, even if she did gain valuable insights from the first exercise. Her concern revolved around whether she would wish to be part of a group:

I don't know whether I'm the sort of person who would enjoy a session with other people or not. This may be due to the fact that because of pressure on my time, I'd find it difficult having to wait my turn. I'd have to help with other people which is, you know, fine – it could be therapeutic and it may be that the other people help with my problem. Not having been to one of these sessions I can't really say; and I just wasn't sure if that would be the sort of thing that I would want to do. So I very much liked the exercise and that made me feel really keen, wondering where would we go from here, but being in a group was honestly less appealing. There's something about sharing myself out the rest of the time, and so it would be a luxury to just be me talking about myself.

In terms of Morag's dilemma of how she can balance her own needs with those of others, this may seem a very predictable reaction and anxiety. It is interesting that Holmes does not identify this as a potential difficulty. It does not, of course, invalidate his view that Morag is suitable for a group, but it suggests that a client's suitability for any approach does not necessarily mean it is the approach the client would choose.

Neither is Morag keen on the idea of a weekend workshop:

The thought of a weekend doing something completely different is quite appealing; but I think I wouldn't want to spend it doing this, although it sounds a sensible way of checking out if it's what you want if you're not sure.

Holmes believes that a single weekend can produce significant therapeutic benefits for some clients. Having seen Morag's rapt attention in the social atom exercise, and heard how significant and effective this one experience had been for her, I can well believe how powerful a weekend could be. Indeed, many therapists can recall weekend workshops they have attended that have had a lasting impact and influence. This may raise the question of whether therapists sometimes need to be more creative; for instance, the social atom exercise could be incorporated into many settings without much difficulty (although you need a large room and lots of chairs of different sizes).

Psychodrama, by definition, is an active approach. Holmes notes how Morag's sentences tail off, and describes how in practice this could be taken up and worked on in the group. He describes how exploring one scene in the client's life can change and develop, and enable the client to go further back into their history. This approach sees the client's history as significant and to be worked with. Holmes feels that Morag's relationship with her father could be an area of potential difficulty in therapy. He introduces the concept of the transferential relationship, again a significant difference from Dryden's position. Although they both take note of the gender difference between the client and the therapist, their emphasis is not the same. Holmes also mentions working with an 'empty chair', which readers may generally associate with a Gestalt approach.

Morag is not convinced by his analysis of her relationship with her father, or its significance either in the past, or of replaying in therapy:

I don't know. I think my relationship with my father has been that his advice is fairly good on things like business problems, and I'd possibly regard a therapist in a similar sort of fashion. What I don't like about my father is his lack of moral behaviour. I get on with him in other ways. I do certainly have mixed feelings towards him now and I suppose he was more or less an absentee father. But that wasn't unusual then. It was how fathers were. A lot of people's fathers of my generation were there but not there.

Morag feels misunderstood by the reference Holmes makes to her 'excluding' her partner from part of the house. She feels her attempt to create a space in the house, which can be untidy and not worry James because it is separate, is misinterpreted:

I suppose I got a little irritated with what was being said in places, after having been very taken with it initially. Some of the facts that he put down about the separate part of house were not right: James isn't excluded, he can come up, but he doesn't like it; he doesn't like it because he thinks it's too untidy.

Holmes is the only therapist to wonder about the role of the stepchildren's father, noting 'his failure to play his role in controlling their behaviour'. He selects this as one of the areas that could usefully be explored further in psychodrama. He again links this to the distance Morag had from her own father, wondering if this realization may help her to deal with the current issues with James. I return below to the question of the stepchildren, and the responses of all the therapists to this issue, noting here that is was important to Morag that Holmes acknowledges the way this also involves their father:

> It does strike a chord. Because of the marriage splitting up he's always wanted to make sure that they feel welcome. But I also think there is a difference between your own children and someone else's children: you always make more allowances for your own children. So it's a combination for him of the fact that they're not there all the time and that they're his, that makes him more accepting of their behaviour. Interestingly, he does from time to time tell our daughter off because she doesn't appreciate what I do for her; but he would never have done that with his own children. So he's quite right to allude to that area.

'Going with the flow' seems a key aspect of this approach. Its flexibility is reflected in the criteria for a successful outcome. It is acknowledged that psychotherapy is a step in the journey of life. It is essentially part of a process of being rather than an event simply in itself. In the end, Morag will be the best judge of progress.

Anthea Millar

Anthea Millar is the only contributor in this volume who describes herself as a counsellor, arguing that there is a lack of a clear distinction between counselling and psychotherapy. Her training was originally with families and emphasized that insight alone is not sufficient. It needs to be accompanied by action. There is a flexibility in an Adlerian approach that allows techniques to be incorporated that may be more obviously linked to other methods (for example, the use of homework assignments and art work).

In her further questions to Morag, Millar was particularly interested to discover the detail and quality of Morag's early relationships and to explore early recollections. As Anthea Millar notes in her account, it was difficult to give her the detailed and focused picture she wished. Although Morag was quite interested in pursuing these early recollections, it seemed her heart was not quite in it. This was verified after she had read Millar's chapter:

> I wasn't sure about early recollections and their significance. I really wasn't too taken with that idea. In a way it's always

quite interesting to see what you can remember, but I don't know how helpful it is.

This led to an interesting although more generalized discussion with Morag on this theme. It became evident that she was not convinced that the cause or the solution to today's problems lies in the past, and that approaches that in her eyes overemphasize the past could alienate her from those therapists. This is a very interesting area to consider, as it involves the match of a therapist and a client, and how this might be achieved. Morag's own words express this:

It doesn't really quite fit or make sense. I suppose I feel they're sort of screw-drivering it in, they're pushing it somewhere it doesn't feel to be, when it's really in the world to some large extent.

This feeling was particularly strong in Morag towards this approach in terms of the attention paid to her position in her family of origin. As Millar explains, the Adlerian approach sees the client's first world of their family as providing a 'life map' that effects their perceptions of later worlds and relationships. However, this did not sit comfortably with Morag, who felt that her family history was being used to *understand* her cleverness and her desire to succeed, rather than *validating* it. Although wanting to explore and understand her enjoyment of challenge, she did not want it explained away; she did not want to lose this aspect of herself, and, correctly or incorrectly, she feared this may be the result:

It would be helpful to see reasons for enjoying challenges, but as this forms part of my enjoyment of life I do not want therapy to diminish my enjoyment. So I would want to direct the dealings rather more towards the mother-hen part of the problem. Putting the desire to achieve down to being third in the family left me feeling that it diminished the struggle to do well; that it dismissed this or made it negative. And why shouldn't I want to do well?

Although Morag feels there is a danger of this approach underplaying both her real achievements and her current external world, it should be noted that Anthea Millar herself clearly and strongly states her own belief that both the inner and the outer world must be recognized and worked with. She stresses how actual tasks can be incorporated into therapy that take real account of current situations and difficulties. It is interesting that this very clear statement was not seen or heard by Morag in her reading of this account. It seemed as if the questions relating to past people and recollections obscured the other aspects of this approach, in a similar way to her great enthusiasm for the social atom test perhaps obscured appreciation of the rest of the psychodrama approach.

It was Millar's understanding of Morag's need to keep moving towards further success in order to exist and be herself that clearly made great sense to her:

> Yes, that really rang a chord and is quite right; but I'm not so sure she really took on board that that is partly because I'm not a man, I've had to work twice as hard to get there.

This issue of how can a woman be successful in a world that is still male-dominated is very important to Morag. She felt that Millar had astutely caught something important here, but also felt the political and structural aspects had been missed.

Morag found the hypotheses that Millar drew up a helpful summary. She explains how in therapy she would share these with her client in order to verify and modify them. Morag's response indicates how this could be a helpful and useful process in helping to focus on relevant areas: clarifying where the therapist had captured a significant theme, while also providing an opportunity for her to reject those that are incorrect or which she does not wish to pursue. Millar describes this as a sharing process and I was struck by how crucial the sharing aspect would be. Within a model such as this, which emphasizes a mutual exploration of these hypotheses, the client is enabled to consider and then accept or reject. This is very different from imposing a view, or an understanding, that suggests that the therapist is an expert who knows best. Of course, there is a danger inherent in *all* therapies (even if some are better at acknowledging it and working with it) of a power imbalance that makes it impossible for some clients to say what they do not agree with or do not like.

Morag's comments illustrate her responses to the hypotheses and how she might want to work with them:

> The one that refers to when things don't go well I start to think 'the grass is greener elsewhere' is right to some extent. But I suppose I'd regard that as a sort of positive thrust rather than delving too deeply into it. So it would be helpful to look at it but not something I'd want to change drastically.

She did not accept the understanding of her recurrent dream:

> She understood my daughter falling over the edge of a balcony as me falling or losing prestige, but that doesn't feel

right. I mean, the sheer panic I feel when I see my daughter in space – I don't think it is to do with me failing but fear of the most precious thing in my life disappearing and not being able to do anything about it. Perhaps this therapist hasn't been a mother, and perhaps only mothers understand that.

How, or if at all, therapists work with, use or interpret dreams is an interesting area to explore. In this instance, a therapist who asked Morag how she understood her dream would have been led into a very different area of her life than the one identified in Millar's hypothesis. A dialogue about the dream, that this hypothesis could initiate, which explores both the therapist's and the client's view, may have opened up significant avenues for further exploration. Millar's recognition of the pull between freedom and responsibility is recognized by Morag as an accurate and helpful observation. It is similar to the conflict Dryden identifies between challenge and responsibility. Therapists who were able to acknowledge these conflicts between different parts of herself made great sense to Morag.

Anthea Millar feels that Morag would be suitable for this Adlerian approach and considers that a cognitive and educative stance would be acceptable to her. Although perhaps not as highly structured as REBT this approach links four goals to four phases of therapy. These are interwoven to create a fluid rather than rigid structure. It is interesting to note that some of the terminology used in the Adlerian chapter is reminiscent of the REBT language used by Windy Dryden, notably the use of 'beliefs' as one major focus. In her use of terms such as 'paraphrasing', 'reflecting' and 'providing empathy', there are again reminders of person-centred terminology. These links to both REBT and person-centred therapy may reflect Millar's own acknowledgement that Adlerian therapy allows many strategies and processes to be incorporated, if it is appropriate to the client.

Millar tells the client that she has access to her own notes if she wishes, and with permission she tapes sessions. The client knows these will be taken to supervision. I wonder how many therapists allow access to notes, and how many explain so clearly that sessions may be taken to a supervisor, since this seems an important ethical and professional issue. A short contract of six sessions is initially agreed. It is worth noting the range of therapist views on this. Millar feels a time-limited contract would be most helpful, both in assisting Morag to maintain focus and because of unclear endings in previous relationships. This latter point seems extremely valid and pertinent in terms of Morag's story. Other therapists (Arthur Jonathan, for instance) opt for an open-ended contract. It is interesting to note a connection between Millar's and Watson's approach to resistance. Watson describes how he would 'go with the flow' if resistance should be in evidence; and Millar describes how she will 'join with the resistance rather than oppose it'.

In Adlerian therapy, as in REBT, successful outcome is linked to achievement of goals and actual behavioural change. As we have seen, the route to these is perceived differently in the two approaches: Adlerian therapy places considerable emphasis on early family relationships in making an assessment. Millar would hope and aim that the changes achieved through therapy would continue thereafter by the client having developed new insights and strategies.

Peter Savage

Peter Savage trained as a hypnotherapist after working in a variety of jobs for a number of years. He obviously values his mixed life experience, feeling that it provides a rich base for therapeutic work. He expresses a strongly held belief that therapy should be popular, accessible and brief, in order that it can reach out to the greatest number of people who are in psychological distress. His training incorporated a wide variety of theoretical approaches without imposing any as the correct and acceptable version. He describes how in the hypnotic state a range of psychological techniques can then be used.

In deciding on the appropriateness of this approach it is necessary, unlike the others described in this book, to check the client's medical history. In this therapy physical factors may be a contraindication, whereas in the others psychological factors are more likely to preclude potential clients. Because of the methods used in hypnotherapy, it is obviously of great importance that the therapist exercises care and responsibility in examining medical history. However, Savage is also interested in the history of the difficulty, including personal and family background. Like Millar, he links Morag's current difficulties to her childhood experiences, although he also recognizes that the qualities arising from this may well have enabled her to be successful. In his assessment, he refers to an Adlerian concept – an example perhaps of the wide theoretical base of his training. He understands some of Morag's difficulties in terms of anxiety; but she herself did not agree with this analysis, particularly in terms of her work situation:

> He says that as a result of anxiety my work is suffering, but this is not so. It's because I spend so much time trying to

keep happy people who are close to me that my work is suffering. This is not anxiety or because of anxiety. But it's more like the core of the problem that in itself needs addressing; so that comment is too simplistic.

Savage wonders about Morag's commitment to her relationship with James and feels that Morag insisted on having a child against his will. This comment aroused an angry and indignant response from Morag:

I was stunned by the comment that I should concentrate on me and my daughter. He couldn't understand what I was doing with my partner in the first place. I think he was pretty brutal. When I first read it I was fairly stunned by the bluntness of his comments. Then I was quite cross at . . . no that's not quite the right word . . . I felt he hadn't understood, that he was oversimplifying and not understanding the mixed feelings that are around. Similarly, his remark about James's lack of affection towards our daughter is not right. He is very affectionate towards her. It's more to do with involvement rather than affection. He's just not right, and again I feel it's an oversimplification: a father may be very fond of, very affectionate towards a child, but still not do very much, may not put it into action. It's actually not an unusual way for fathers to behave.

Like the other therapists, Peter Savage feels that Morag is a good candidate for psychotherapy and identifies some factors that he considers would enable her to use hypnotherapy well, notably her ability to become absorbed in an activity. He makes an interesting comment that most mothers are effective primitive hypnotherapists, Morag's mother being no exception. He is the only therapist to suggest that another therapist should work with Morag concurrently. He would want to suggest someone with specific training in couples work, although he does not discuss the issues of her partner's dislike of therapy and Morag's decision not to involve him. He does not make it clear whether he envisages that this other person should work on the relationship via Morag or whether he is assuming (although it would be an incorrect assumption) that James would wish to be involved. Like Dryden, he locates the relationship as one key area of difficulty, but he feels that this should be addressed elsewhere, and sees this as an intrinsic part of the overall process.

Peter Savage's suggestion of concurrent therapy raises an interesting and pertinent question for therapists to consider: Would they see it as appropriate and helpful to divide the work in this way?

Would they see it, for instance, as diluting the therapeutic potency: interfering with the transference; creating boundary difficulties; creating and colluding with splitting? Or would they see it as a sensible and creative use of available resources that enables different aspects of the difficulty to be dealt with effectively by practitioners with specific skills? I suspect the responses to these questions would vary enormously between different therapeutic orientations.

A very clear difference in this approach from the others described in this book is the emphasis placed on relaxation, breathing and bodily tension, and working directly with these aspects of the self. Before reading Savage's account, readers may not have recognized that the hypnosis itself is a medium through which other forms of interventions can be utilized. In his account, the two methods cited are cognitive behaviour therapy and direct suggestion. Savage argues that the power of suggestion through repetition is an effective method of changing behaviour. Although family history is considered, the primary focus of the work is not on understanding and working with the past, but on shifting attitudes and behaviour in the present. His method of so doing is very particular, but the emphasis is similar to that seen in the chapters on REBT and Adlerian therapy.

Savage is the only therapist to incorporate the use of a tape made solely for the individual client. Although other therapists expect clients to undertake tasks between sessions, this is a very specific method. I imagine this could be quite a powerful experience for the client, to feel that her own unique needs are being thought about and responded to in this way. Some therapists from different theoretical backgrounds may regard this as an effective way of enabling the client to hold or internalize the therapist in his or her absence. The tape could be understood as acting as a transitional object and could create an attachment to, and dependence on, the therapist. However, these concepts suggest the centrality of the relationship to the therapeutic method, yet this does not appear to be the case with this approach – indeed, Peter Savage talks about 'undesirable dependence upon the therapist'.

Morag has mixed feelings about this therapy. This may reflect Peter Savage's own recognition that there may be more to the presentation than is at first obvious. He notes how Morag's use of terminology may suggest she is aware of other layers and levels. Morag herself says that:

There is an appeal in this approach because it's short, but I also feel that it might not work because it wouldn't get to grips with what it's really about. So, yes, on the one hand I felt very positive about this, but I then wondered if it could get to the root of the problem, because if he sees the problem as just dealing with the symptoms I think it could be a waste of time: it's important to understand it all and if I don't get to understand what it is about it won't help. It'll just keep on coming back. I found the idea of relaxation very boring; and if this was an essential part of therapy it would fail, because again it deals with symptoms and not the cause. But if it did work I have to say it would appeal greatly – the speed of therapy in particular would appeal.

It should be said that throughout Peter Savage notes that if Morag were in therapy with him the methods used would be open to mutual discussion and decision. In this instance, if Morag remained so unconvinced by the use of relaxation, they might decide together that this approach is not the best for her. On the other hand, she is clearly attracted to a method that quickly gets hold of the problem, so I can imagine that she may try it first. Depending on her initial reaction she would then reach a decision.

In terms of successful outcome, Savage feels that the best judge of this is Morag herself, noting that we are all able to judge whether we feel well or unwell. He is not convinced that more seemingly objective measures of physiological stress are more reliable or problem-free. However, he does use other scales of measurement to assess progress. There is a clear difference between approaches: some therapists use these formal measures of outcome; others regard outcome as subjective and not accessible to formal measurement.

Roxane Agnew

Roxane Agnew trained as a clinical psychologist with an emphasis on cognitive behavioural approaches. While recognizing the value of this approach, she also felt that it lacked an awareness of the significance of emotion, both within personal experience and within therapy. In discovering focused expressive psychotherapy (FEP), she found an approach which offered a framework that actively incorporated and validated emotional experience, while also acknowledging the relevance of cognitive structures.

When working in FEP, Agnew notes process as well as content. In the further information she requests from Morag, she both explores how she normally expresses emotions, and then explains how these and other aspects of the self will be influenced by rules and scripts (reminiscent of transactional analysis terminology) learned from significant others. This leads to her asking Morag about how her parents expressed their emotions. As we have seen, Morag has queried the value of looking at past relationships with some of the other therapists, but she seemed to find it more acceptable when it was within this framework which explained its relevance. Morag's own words best express this difference:

> Several of them refer back to my childhood, but in a sense they are just looking at little cameos and I didn't feel they had any great significance, although it was interesting to look back. But when she talked about how my mother dealt with things and how my father dealt with things, I can see how this would have had an effect on me.

Agnew continues to explore Morag's feelings in more depth, moving this into the area of her relationship with her partner, James, and her ex-partner, Carl. She checks out if the termination of pregnancy is a problem area. Morag's response to Roxane Agnew's awareness of the need to work on feelings was very positive; indeed, she seemed extremely relieved at being given permission to feel:

> When I read them through I was making notes on them and I've put down 'permission to feel!' – and the exclamation mark says it all. My feeling about her was that she did say it's OK to feel and that was a weight lifted off. That was really appealing to me because I think she's right in that I do suppress feelings that I have. Also, she seemed to deal with it in what I thought was quite a methodical way – taking one area of unfinished business and taking it through. That would appeal, it's the way I would try and work through a problem anyway, so it also appealed to the logical in me. It felt like that within a structure I could feel things in a safe way.

It was evident that Morag needed both confirmation and affirmation that she had a right to have feelings and express them, but that she also needed a clear and firm structure to do this within safely.

Agnew stresses the importance in FEP of process diagnosis – the therapist being guided by what emerges from the client. Interpretation of the material is therefore seen as inappropriate. She is aware of details in Morag's presentation, for instance, noting her tendency to laugh off an emotion. Morag found this helpful, and it enabled her to consider for herself what this might be about:

> She identified things that I found interesting, like the little laugh that I have. I now notice that I do this, and I notice

that my mother also does that: she does it if she gets
embarrassed about things, or if she makes statements about
what she wants, so I can now see where that comes from
and what it may be about.

Agnew sees FEP as being particularly helpful for people who suppress or over-control emotions, and as such feels that it would be
particularly appropriate for Morag. She cites examples of how Morag
is aware of her own over-control. Morag agreed with her assessment,
although also expressed some anxiety over what may happen if she
did not suppress her feelings in the world outside of therapy:

I do suppress how I feel. I do it so that I won't hurt other
people. I'm not sure if you start expressing feelings that may
hurt other people you'll necessarily feel much better. Because,
although you may have got your own feelings out, you may
have hurt them in the process. But it would be good to have
a place where you don't have to worry about that.

Agnew recognizes Morag's negative feelings towards James but
also acknowledges the strength of their relationship. In discussing
all the chapters with Morag, it became evident that she was relieved
that this had been recognized by Agnew. However, she did feel that
linking the possibility of unfinished business with Carl to difficulty
in fully investing in this relationship with James was not entirely
correct:

She may be right but that's not how I see it. I think what
she had missed, and she wasn't the only one, was very
simply how very special that relationship had been.

Roxane Agnew identifies markers (process indicators) that will
indicate the course of the therapeutic work by identifying difficult,
painful and conflictual areas. A contract for a specific number of
sessions will be offered and Morag will be encouraged to note and
express what she is feeling; the strategies she employs to deal with
these, while understanding their origins. Each session will move
through a series of steps. In these ways, the therapy is both structured and focused. There are also overtones of Winnicott as Agnew
talks about therapy being 'a safe place to play'. She picks up on
Morag's statements about other people needing to change, and
wonders if Morag may be able to turn this around. Instead of waiting for others to change, she could change herself in relation to
them. Morag found this an interesting idea which resonated with
her own experience:

Yes, that does have an appeal, because I realize one can't change the other person, unless they want to, and I would like to be able not to get so bothered by it. I think this would especially help with James, as I feel so frustrated by the way he doesn't take positive action – I almost give up with him. I don't mean that literally, but that's the feeling I have – there's almost no point in discussing the problem again, because I know I'll get nowhere with it. I can't change him, so I'm only left with changing my own reactions.

Some readers may feel a sense of unease at these words. To therapists who work with women who feel they have few choices in life but to accept what is offered, however unsatisfactory, it may seem that this is very much an adjustment model. It could be understood as suggesting that women should change themselves, rather than that unacceptable situations should be tackled or challenged. As Roxane Agnew talks of empowerment and choice, this is highly unlikely to be her view. However, it is a concern worth noting, particularly as Morag herself made reference to it:

It is maybe what I need to do, to make changes in myself, but what it doesn't deal with is the wider issues for women, and the problem of women achieving in society. But actually it doesn't in any of them – none of the therapists have looked at that.

Agnew, like other therapists, sees successful outcome as best gauged by the client as the expert on her own experience, but she sees evaluation of the therapeutic process as an integral and ongoing part of the work. Again in common with some of the other therapies described in this book, this will occur against the backdrop of goals that have been agreed. Morag had mixed feelings about the value of goal setting:

I do see goals primarily as being helpful to the therapist so they know when it's ended. My feeling is that it's a bit neat, because as you start to look at things you'll understand it differently and the goals would keep on changing as you go along. So it might be a waste of time saying I want to sort this particular issue because it might actually turn out to be another one. It might be hard to say that. I suppose I wonder who you're setting goal posts for.

Although Morag had reservations about some aspects of this therapy, she nevertheless felt that out of the six this would be the approach and person she would be most likely to choose. She explained why:

I was trying to work out how I felt when I'd left here last time (when we had met to discuss some of the chapters). It was like having watched a film, an emotional film, and it takes you through lots of emotions, and when you come out at the end you feel sort of drained, as if you've been asleep for a long time, but it's all so absorbed you and got through to you somehow, and been important and worthwhile. In a sense, reading through hers I feel a similar sort of feeling which suggests that she actually does get to more of the areas and provides a focus for what I'm needing. She touches something, gets near to something – yes, that's it. She involves the past, but in a way that actually seems relevant to me now; she gets hold of the right bits, she gets hold of what I'm really saying, she's responding to me rather than just using her approach. It felt as if she were tuned in to me. It is an organized approach but one that gives space to go through things.

Arthur Jonathan

Arthur Jonathan's existential therapy focuses on the client's experience of being and relating in the world. Therefore, relational aspects of the client's world are explored and worked with – a significant difference from approaches that focus on cognitions or behaviour and aim to produce actual and measurable changes in these. It is the process that is central in existential therapy, rather than deciding at an early stage on the desirable outcome. Another key difference is that Jonathan offers interpretations in an attempt to clarify the client's experience. There is an emphasis on the therapist listening carefully and non-judgementally, and in doing so taking care that his own views and biases do not impede the process. As with Millar's account, there are some similarities to the ideas and terminoloy of the person-centred approach. This may reflect that the core conditions of the person-centred approach are seen as *necessary* by many practitioners, the major disagreement being over whether or not they are *sufficient*. Jonathan describes how a close engagement in dialogue with the client takes place, the quality of the relationship being the core of the process. This therapy has a strong philosophy of 'being with' rather than 'doing to'.

Jonathan is concerned to look further at the relationship with James and is the only therapist to wonder why they have not married when Morag had wanted marriage with her previous partner. In the light of her response to this, he wonders if there may be more here that needs examining. This did make sense to Morag, although she felt it was not a straightforward issue:

> If I'm honest it's because I very much felt Carl was the ideal
> partner for me and I guess when you've lost the ideal
> partner . . . maybe I don't feel now that James is as ideal for
> me as he was. So he was quite perceptive in picking that
> out. But the other thing is that I believe that having a child
> with somebody is a more binding contract than marriage
> ever will be, because the commitment in having a child is so
> great that it means more than getting married.

Jonathan's discussion of Morag's not wishing to marry James aroused strong feelings in her. While recognizing that there might indeed be some aspects of this that it would be helpful to explore, she felt that his comments on her 'fear of marriage' are not correct and she wondered if this carries an underlying assumption:

> He comments on my 'fear' of marriage and the 'threat' of
> James. That's completely wrong and I think there may be
> huge assumptions underneath it, for instance, that marriage
> in itself is desirable and a good thing. Well . . . where do we
> start on that one?

Morag also felt that the reference to her having no commitment to helping James was wrong: that much of her life is in fact devoted to this, and that this is an essential part of her dilemma. She also wondered at Jonathan's comment regarding her responsibility and commitment towards her stepchildren:

> The comments on the children seem to entirely miss the
> point that they are James's children. What about his
> responsibility towards them? The question of stepchildren
> is a really difficult and complex one – what level of
> responsibility do you take on for children who already have
> two parents? How do you fit into an existing equation? I do
> feel this could be very stereotyping of women: would the
> same comments be made if the genders were reversed? I
> think he dismissed something that is incredibly complex,
> almost one of the most difficult situations in life to cope
> with for anybody. It would be difficult to be in therapy with
> someone who didn't understand the nuances of that and I
> don't want the responsibility in therapy of having to explain
> it. It's an incredibly thorny issue and I almost feel that until
> you've been in that situation yourself you don't realize the
> feelings that arise.

Of course, if Morag was in therapy with Arthur Jonathan, particularly given the emphasis in this approach on the quality of the relationship, it could be expected that this area would engender active dialogue and be worked with. This would assume sufficient trust on Morag's behalf to express this feeling as indignantly to her therapist as she did to me, and whether or not she would feel it was appropriate for her to have to do so. Although this comment from Morag is here responding to Arthur Jonathan, Morag was concerned that readers understood that she felt it actually applied to all the therapists: that the whole issue of reconstituted families was never sufficiently recognized. This does pose a challenge to therapies and therapists: Are they sufficiently aware of changing family structures and the sociological and psychological implications of these changes? There is a danger that both policy makers and the caring professions conceptualize within a framework that no longer exists.

Like Roxane Agnew, Arthur Jonathan wonders about the significance for Morag of the termination of her pregnancy. Given the degree of difficulty and loss this is known to create for many women, it is puzzling that some therapists did not refer to this event. Jonathan is also interested in pursuing Morag's feelings about growing old with James, and what that represents to her. He feels that this is an area that needs further exploration, as does her own family history.

In his assessment of Morag and her difficulties, Jonathan notes that she feels society should cater for women and children, and that her response to its failure to do so is to take action herself. This is a very accurate reflection of her view of the world and the part she can play in it. However, Morag viewed this aspect of herself positively, and was less sure that this is the therapist's perception:

> I did note that he picked up my expectation that society
> should cater for women with children and that my strategy
> is to lodge a protest. Yes. He has got something there in the
> way I feel and the way I go about trying to alter things or
> help in a very small way. I'm not sure he thinks it's so good
> to feel and act like that. I felt he was being accurate but at
> the same time I thought he might be being critical, rather
> than saying, 'Good for you'.

It is, of course, difficult to know what meaning was intended by Arthur Jonathan, although his phrase 'with a hint of self-righteousness' may imply criticism rather than validation. He explores the process by which she left her former partner, examines her new current relationship with James and how this creates conflict and difficulties for her in relation to Paula. Morag feels that the situation

with Paula is problematic, does cause her difficulty and certainly
arouses strong feelings in her:

> It does irritate me that his links with his ex-wife and his
> family are very strong and he is so beholden to them . . . if
> they say jump, he jumps. They manage to make him feel
> guilty, so in a way I feel he isn't mine anyway, as at that
> point he's not really with me; and as such I'd rather stand
> back a bit.

Although Arthur Jonathan generally feels that Morag could work
within this approach, he does see some contraindications, wondering if she may be too set in her perspective for her to be willing to
be challenged. He also comments on the selective way she responded
to his questions. It was fascinating to observe a reciprocal process
emerging when Morag was discussing this contribution. She questioned whether he would be too set in his perspective. She felt that
he selected and interpreted parts of her story to fit his way of thinking. It seems they both had similar doubts about one another, although at other points they were each able to express positive feelings
about the other. Morag explained what she meant:

> He comments on 'withdrawing and taking unilateral action'
> and mentions 'compromise, negotiation and adaptability and
> my need for recognition'. It does feel sexist; I suspect it
> might be OK for a man to be unilateral. And the comments
> on my need for recognition gave me the impression that I
> was having a little moan, which annoyed me because I know
> I am good – I've won four major contracts this year and why
> should I feel embarrassed by that? There was a suggestion of:
> 'Are you sure you haven't got delusions of grandeur?' I
> sensed in relation to Carl, something of the attitude of, 'So
> what, he had an affair, you gave up a lot because of one
> action that you were particularly intolerant of'. I could work
> with this chap in that he comes over as gentle and kind, but
> I'm worried that he wants me to adapt to mother-hen; it's
> very chauvinistic. I felt there was a danger of him reinforcing
> stereotypes rather than helping me to challenge them. I
> know it would always be possible to work with someone on
> just those issues, but my fear would be that there would be
> bits of the map that couldn't be covered. I don't think he is
> used to working with women who are struggling to find their
> place in the world.

I was left with a strong impression that if Morag and Arthur
Jonathan were to work together, it would indeed be a mutually

challenging dialogue in which these issues would need the most careful of attention. This is not to say that this might not be a very rewarding therapeutic encounter for both. My concern would be that if in any therapy Morag had to fight her corner too much, and explain too much, there might not be room for the needier side of her (that Jonathan identifies) to emerge. However, Jonathan himself emphasizes that in this approach it is crucial that both participants in the process are able to be challenged and face difficulties; and that both need an openness that can result in change on both sides. In this sense, Arthur Jonathan's approach and conceptualization, and the vigour of Morag's response, could either prove a powerful combination or could make it a non-starter.

Summary

Morag found the experience of participating in this book an interesting one. As already noted, she found something in all the contributions that were of value, and gave her food for thought. She also recognized and appreciated the time and effort expended by all the therapists and was concerned that they should all know this. She was also left with many important questions about the nature of therapy that are worth further discussion. I have insufficient space to explore these in any detail, but Morag's own words highlight significant areas, and serve as a basis in themselves for further questions and discussion.

A crucial theme for Morag related to women's issues generally. She did not feel that the therapists had given sufficient attention to these areas, or were sufficiently aware of them as significant:

> I think a lot of my issues are women's issues and I don't feel that was picked up enough for me. Nobody reinforced my right to be out there in the world, or looked at the problem of being in the world as a woman, whilst also having to do all the other bits. So in a sense there was a danger that they could take away the positive aspects of my life, by explaining my success away. They didn't pick up the structural issues of what it's like to be a woman in today's society and having to meet lots of different demands and how you balance that. It's so much a background to women's existence as a whole; it's so insidious, if you like. I don't think anyone has dealt with that adequately. It is a very core issue, the core of existence and maybe it is fundamental to the problem. My feeling overall is that people latched on too much to me

wanting to achieve things and I worried that I would end up worse off – that I would end up feeling that the only reason I like to achieve is because I was the third in a family of four, or whatever. That may be the reason initially but it negates the feeling you get when you did do something well and the pleasure you get in doing it well. So I was worried that I would end up with my achievements denigrated and no particular help in the areas that I wanted help in.

Morag also felt that no-one explored sufficiently the difficulty of incorporating stepchildren on an occasional, albeit regular, basis into a woman's life and world. We had a lengthy discussion on this. I had commented to Morag in the last stages of our meetings that I had been interested to note that none of the therapists in their further questions to her had asked how she felt when the stepchildren had been with her a while. In other words, they had all picked up on the point of their arrival in the home, and her immediate feelings then; but none had explored the ongoing process of their stay. I was aware of how visiting stepchildren can commonly create for the step-parent a feeling of invasion: there are the continual emotional and practical adjustments to make every time a child comes and goes, and the possibility, if not inevitability, of strong feelings being aroused. It is as if the completed jigsaw puzzle of the home has to be taken apart and rearranged to make room for the new pieces. This made great sense to Morag and it transpired that had the therapists picked up the process rather than the event, a very different picture would have emerged:

Although when the children walk in through the door I feel very aggressive towards them, it gets much easier and I enjoy them being around, and we all have some fun. It's just the initial feeling of invasion because I can enjoy them being there. It seems to be more to do with this coming and going. There is some jealousy there and if you're going to look into that you'd need a gentle approach and to be very careful because it's a sensitive and complex area. Some of the comments made about me and the stepchildren could undermine and have put a heavy guilt trip on me. I think the complexity wasn't recognized or acknowledged, and I think that was because they didn't really understand those complexities and nuances. A friend said to me something that none of the therapists picked up which was very helpful – that in my childhood everyone knew where they slotted in; the hierarchy was clear and perhaps what I resent when the children arrive is that they don't know what their situation is, where they fit in, and the fit takes time to work out.

Some of the male therapists had discussed the implications of her seeing a man. Morag had mixed feelings about this, and it is interesting that she comments on her own tendency to stereotype:

> The only problem I'd see in working with a man as opposed to a woman is that they may not pick up on the women's issues although, as I've said, in fact *none* of them did. Perhaps I'm making sexist statements here, when I also say that maybe men understand work challenges more than women. You tend to want someone who is also going to understand the demands of that world, and the need to strive to do well. It would have been nice to have had a feminist represented here as well, just to see what the difference would have been.

Morag also expressed concern that as a lay person she would have had little idea before participating in this book of the different therapies that exist. She herself saw 'huge differences between them' and felt strongly that finding the right therapist was crucial, as 'some might end up antagonizing rather than helping'. She clearly felt that finding a therapist with the right fit for the individual was crucial but sometimes difficult. She found the introductory statements from the therapists describing their training, experience and philosophy extremely helpful and informative. She asked me if therapists would routinely provide potential clients with this thumbnail sketch. Morag felt that clients should feel they have a right to choose their therapist and to know this background information, and wondered if 'clients going for therapy realize that they have all these different options'. It is relevant to consider further to what extent clients seen in the public sector, as opposed to the private, have any choice at all. Morag's experience was that this is most important. It is also necessary to refer to an anxiety that Morag expressed, one that should always be taken seriously by therapists:

> One of the things I worry about is that therapy or greater understanding may have a negative effect on what I regard as the positive things in my life, and that other things won't change. So I would worry that I might walk away with less than I had before.

I should add that despite this concern and other questions that have been discussed briefly, Morag was positive about having participated in this project and at this stage she decided that she would like to enter therapy. We discussed at some length whom she would like to see. What was clear was that she wanted a therapist who had a particular interest in women's issues, and that she would like the option of working in a short-term focused way. Her busy life gave short-term work a particular appeal. She also recognized that until therapy was under way, she might not know whether she would like it to be longer. I referred her to a woman in her own locality, one who describes herself as a feminist psychodynamic therapist and whom I knew to be very aware of the implications for women of complex family structures and relationships. Having come this far with Morag, neither I nor the reader will know the outcome of this therapy. What we are left with is a clear impression from Morag that her involvement in the process of this book gave her valuable insights into the therapeutic world, and into the choices available within it.

CHARLIE – AN UNWANTED CHILD?
Michael Jacobs (ed.)

'All the while I very much got the impression when I was young that my mother didn't love me and doesn't love me. I think of myself as unlovable . . .'

These are Charlie's opening words to her potential therapist. Six therapists are given the opportunity of assessing Charlie: What do they wish to know about her? How do they understand her? How might they work with her? And what outcome can they predict for her as a result of therapy?

In this fascinating book – which starts with Charlie's own story – the reader has the chance to see six different therapists at work, drawing on the same initial material from the one real client. The similarities and differences between therapies and therapists are highlighted. And at the end the reader is able to enter Charlie's experience of the process, and decide with her, which one she might choose in her search for a therapist.

This highly original volume will appeal to a wide range of students and practitioners involved in counselling and psychotherapy, particularly those interested in comparing different therapeutic approaches.

Contents
The editors: in search of the client – Charlie: an unwanted child? – The reader's response – Cassie Cooper: Kleinian psychotherapy – Phil Lapworth: transactional analysis – Frank Margison: psychoanalytic psychotherapy – Alix Pirani: humanistic-transpersonal psychotherapy – Antony Ryle: cognitive-analytic therapy – Claire Wintram: feminist group therapy – Michael Jacobs and Charlie: review and response.

Contributors
Cassie Cooper, Phil Lapworth, Frank Margison, Alix Pirani, Antony Ryle, Claire Wintram.

176pp   0 335 19199 1 (paperback)

PETA - A FEMINIST'S PROBLEM WITH MEN
Moira Walker (ed.)

'I've got a problem with men . . . I don't know whether it's a problem with other things as well . . . I am afraid of what men represent . . . I feel they have more power.'

This is how Peta begins to tell her story to her potential therapist. Six therapists are given the opportunity of assessing Peta: What do they wish to know about her? How do they understand her? How might they work with her? And what outcome can they predict for her as a result of therapy?

In this fascinating book – which starts with Peta's own story – the reader has the chance to see six different therapists at work, drawing on the same initial material from the one real client. The similarities and differences between therapies and therapists are highlighted. And at the end the reader is able to enter Peta's experience of the process, and decide with her, which one she might choose in her search for a therapist.

This highly original volume will appeal to a wide range of students and practitioners involved in counselling and psychotherapy, particularly those interested in comparing different therapeutic approaches.

Contents
The editors: in search of the client – Peta: a feminist's problem with men – The reader's response – Jennifer Mackewn: Gestalt psychotherapy – Judy Moore: person-centred psychotherapy – John Ormrod: cognitive behaviour therapy – John Rowan: humanistic and integrative psychotherapy – Maye Taylor: feminist psychotherapy – Christine Wood: art therapy – Moira Walker and Peta: review and response.

Contributors
Jennifer Mackewn, Judy Moore, John Ormrod, John Rowan, Maye Taylor, Christine Wood.

168pp   0 335 19223 8 (paperback)